Living D

A Beginner's Guide To Celebrate Life The Danish Way, Eliminate Stress With The Rules of Hygge (Hygge, Cozy Living, Contentment, Simply Living, Stress-Free)

Astrid S. Nielsen

Living Danishly: A Beginner's Guide To Celebrate Life The Danish Way, Eliminate Stress With The Rules of Hygge (Hygge, Cozy Living, Contentment, Simply Living, Stress-Free)

Table of Contents

Book 1 - Hygge 01

A Beginner's Guide To Celebrate Life The Danish Way (Denmark, Simple Things, Mindfulness, Connection, Introduction)

1 - Introduction

Everyone dreams of living the perfect life. Of course, there are varying definitions of what this perfect life is. For most, it means having a successful job, owning a big home in a fancy neighborhood, and driving the latest luxury automobile.

Others, on the other hand, agree that the perfect life simply means spending quality time with the special people in their lives. Regardless of how one imagines his perfect life to be, it is undeniable that much of it is attributable to the positive feeling it gives – happiness.

Happiness, however, is another intriguing concept. Although not entirely foreign, not a lot of people know what it actually means, or how it feels. Because of this mystery, people are willing to exhaust all efforts to find it. Most of the time, they rely on the definition portrayed by the media.

However, too much reliance on these media messages results in the encouragement of materialism and perfectionism. And when that happens, a person ends up working tirelessly just to make sure he is able to afford life's many luxuries – whether it genuinely makes him happy or not.

In reality, happiness doesn't work that way. True happiness

cannot be measured by its manifestations in the physical world. It is an internal occurrence; something which can only be felt. It makes a person loved, content, and accepted.

But, if there are people who have unlocked the secret to happiness, these are the Danes. Consistently recognized as the happiest people on earth, the descendants of the once-feared Vikings live life differently than the rest of the world. The secret lies in their love for food, music, and dance. It's in the way they deal with people. It lies in hygge.

Hygge doesn't have an exact English translation, but the word is often described as the state of coziness or intimacy. Properly pronounced as "hoo-gah", people's fascination towards this Danish concept has rapidly grown in the past years. And it greatly deserves the recognition.

After all, it has beneficial effects, including lowered levels of stress, increased feelings of support, and an improved over-all well-being. When all these positive effects are put together, a person develops a greater appreciation towards life.

Thus, one of the key components to the envied Danish happiness is hygge. But how does hygge work, exactly? It is an agreed fact that in order to understand hygge, it is best to experience it. Since it deals with how the Danes live their lives, it is recommended to welcome it into one's life as well.

Fortunately, hygge can be learned. It is the result of a conscious choice to always see the positive side in everything, and to choose to do it relentlessly. Through this conscious effort to change, people slowly develop the mindfulness needed to fully comprehend this concept. After all, hygge is not just an emotion or a feeling – it's a philosophy; it's a way of life.

Aside from mindfulness, another key component of hygge is simple living. Simple living doesn't mean absolutely letting go of material riches, but it has something more to do with living comfortably. When one goes beyond what is needed to live comfortably, then he is already living excessively. And when that happens, the essence of hygge is believed to be lost.

Another notable component of hygge is connection. This is the kind of genuine bond between persons to help them strengthen and develop their relationship. Connecting with others not only builds networks and support groups, but also develops a sense of belonging. This, in turn, boosts a person's self-worth, and thus adding to his overall happiness meter.

Thus, it cannot be denied that the Danes value comfort, connection, and internal awareness. When all these components are present, one is able to experience the genuine bliss brought about by hygge.

Luckily, one does not have to travel all the way to Denmark to experience this phenomenon. Neither does one have to acquire a new set of skills nor use any equipment, since these are all naturally hardwired into the DNA of any human being.

Nonetheless, embracing a new lifestyle will not be easy. Although, possible, it is not easy. It requires letting go of what one has already grown accustomed to. It also means reorienting the brain to accept that there is in a new way of living life. It involves both internal and external changes, and that can be quite exhausting. But when these changes seem to be too overwhelming, just embrace it.

Remember, celebrating life the Danish way opens the doors to experiencing true happiness. However, the journey may be faced with numerous challenges. And that is why, like many other goals in life, it is important to keep in mind to focus on the goal and its long-term result rather than be dragged down by the challenges.

2 - Denmark

Overview

The small Scandinavian country of Denmark is located in Northern Europe where it is bordered by Norway, Sweden, and Germany. Formally known as the Kingdom of Denmark, this small country has a total land area of 42, 924 square kilometers, comprising of the Jutland peninsula and an archipelago of over 400 named islands.

Although often referred to as the smallest Nordic country, Denmark is anything but small. Its history is one of the most interesting in the world, which attracts historians from all over the world.

Additionally, much of its structures from the Bronze Age and the Middle Ages still stand today, attracting hundreds of thousands of tourists every year. Its prime location boasts a 7,400-kilometer coastline, picturesque sand spits, and breathtaking rock formations, making it the perfect summer destination for those in the neighboring countries.

But, what truly attracts visitors to keep coming back to Denmark is its culture. The relaxed atmosphere throughout the country adds to the country's overall unique charm. Others refer to it as a certain Danish hospitality, while others readily identify it as hygge.

And with the hygge lifestyle slowly gaining recognition in the international scene, a growing number of visitors go to this country just to immerse themselves into this life-changing experience. Once they get a taste of hygge, they embrace it as a part of their lives and try to bring it home.

To completely understand the concept of hygge, much emphasis must be given to the way the Danish people celebrate life. It is important to learn about Denmark – its history, climate, and culture, and how all these factors collectively contribute to the hygge lifestyle.

History

The first known record of inhabitants in Denmark is dated as far back as 12500 BC. Back then, much of the Scandinavian region was blanketed in ice, except for some parts of Denmark. By the end of the ice age, the land mass became the new home of reindeer and elks, making it very attractive to the first hunters.

Of course, back then, Denmark was not yet archipelago, and much of Europe was connected by land bridges. That is why these hunters often migrated from place to place.

Because of this prehistoric mass migration, the area didn't have any permanent settlers until around 6,000 BC. This was also attributable to the fact that as the sea levels rose higher, islands started to form. It made traveling challenging. Nonetheless, the hunters began to adapt a seafood based diet which eventually encouraged permanent settlement.

Records also reveal show that the early Danish settlers of the Stone and Bronze Ages were inventive. They already had intricate agricultural inroads, and were already familiar with social stratification – they already divided their people into classes.

Without a doubt, however, Denmark is best known in history for being home to the mighty Vikings. The Vikings are recognized for their fearless outlook and mastery of navigation and shipbuilding. There were also skilled fighters and were adept in strategizing.

In fact, these are the same qualities which helped them conquer a large portion of Europe. True enough, they were a force to be reckoned with during their time. Additionally, it was also during the Viking Age that the name "Denmark" first came to be. It is believed to have appeared as carved on the famous mounds in the town of Jelling.

When the age of the Vikings came to an end, Denmark was already one of the major superpowers in Europe. Much has happened to the country between the 13th and 17th centuries. Denmark faced by many trials and celebrated many triumphs. It was also from the late 1300s until the early 1900s that the country was able to showcase its prowess in the field of architecture and design.

Most of its notable castles and manors were constructed during this time. Some of its most iconic are the Nyborg Castle, Castle of Koldinghaus, and the Kronborg Castle, while those reflecting the rich culture of Denmark include Egeskov Castle, Frederiksborg Palace, Rosenborg Castle, and Christiansborg Castle.

Today, Denmark's size has greatly reduced, compared to how it was 400 years ago. But, it certainly has not lost its grandeur. It boasts one of the most stable economies and continues to contribute in the fields of design, architecture, and green technology.

They continue to be innovative, just as their ancestors were. It is also envied for its comprehensive social welfare scheme, particularly in the fields of education, employment benefits, and health services.

Modern-day Denmark remains relatively peaceful despite the many battles it fought in the past. If there is anything that its eventful history is telling people, it's that the Danes know how to adapt to the different situations in life. This helped them to rise above hardships, and to genuinely celebrate success. This is the quality which made them who they are today: the happiest people on earth.

Geography and Climate

The small Scandinavian country of Denmark is located in Northern Europe where it is bordered by the North and the Baltic Seas. Its archipelago is composed of about 443 named islands, the biggest of which are Zealand and Funen, where much of its population resides.

Given its layout as an archipelago, Denmark boasts an estimated total coastline of about 8,750 kilometers, making it home to some of the best beaches in Europe. It is even said that nowhere in Denmark is too far from the sea – making it a prime summer destination for its neighboring countries.

Transportation is not an issue in Denmark. Much of its inter-island transportation is via sea-based vehicles; and since these are descendants of the innovative seafarers of the 9th century, there is nothing to worry about.

Nonetheless, two of Denmark's biggest islands are connected by the Great Belt Bridge for convenience. Traveling to the nearby Sweden and the Jutland by car is also made possible via the Oresund Bridge and the Little Belt Bridge respectively.

Although Denmark has embraced industrialization and urbanization over the years, it is an undeniable fact that the area is composed of flat and arable lands. This makes it soil fertile for agricultural purposes.

Its prime location has also provided it with breathtaking natural formations like The Hammer, the White Cliffs of Mon, and the breathtaking landscapes of the island of Fur. Other notable natural spots include the dunes of Rabjerg Mile, the Rubjerg Knot, the Mols Bjerge National Park, and the sand spit of The Branch.

Like most countries located in the northern hemisphere,

Denmark enjoys a generally temperate climate. Winters are often mild, while summers are comparatively cool.

However, this location also means long winter nights, where the sun often rises at around 8:45 in the morning, and begins to set as early as 3:45 in the afternoon. Most people often hate these harsh winters because of its gloominess and biting cold. And this reflects yet another admirable trait of the Danish people.

Danes do not allow themselves to be affected by these long, dark nights. They have embraced it as a part of their lives. Instead of sulking over the early sunset, they have successfully incorporated it into their lifestyle. In fact, it is believed that the presence of hygge is at its peak during the winter season.

They acknowledge the harsh weather as the perfect excuse to stay indoors and enjoy the company of their loved ones. Again, this positive outlook in life forms another aspect as to why the Danish people are among the happiest in the world.

Culture and Hygge

Although already part of the past, Denmark's rich history is reflected in its interesting and diverse culture. Each of its towns has its own unique charm, which perfectly depicts the story it went through. Take its capital city of Copenhagen, for example. This former Viking village is the perfect proof of the country's successful transition towards urbanization.

A lot like how it was in the past, much of Copenhagen's tourism and economy still revolves around its ports, harbors, and canals – even its most photographed panoramas are the views of the waterfront areas of the city.

Nonetheless, they made sure that its infrastructures would embrace and adapt to its changing times. It ensures that everyone will be provided with what they need in order to live in the present.

Aside from the country's successful transition towards industrialization and urbanization, the Danes are also known for their contributions in the field of Science. Numerous renowned Danes excelled in the scientific fields of physics, astronomy, and nano-technology with names like Tycho Brahe, Niels Bohr, and Ludwig Colding.

It is also home to some of the best philosophers, authors, composers, and poets the world has ever known. In fact, much acknowledgment is given to Soren Kierkegaard for his contribution towards existential philosophy, and to Hans Christian Anderson for his numerous fairy tales. Thus, it is undeniable that Denmark is a country whose culture revolves around a shared love for learning and cultivating the arts.

Much of Denmark's culture can also be attributed to its temperate climate. More specifically, you have to look at the long and cold winters. Since prehistoric times, Scandinavian countries are known to consider midwinter as one their most important seasons.

During this time, families would gather together and enjoy each other's company. This gathering does not have to be fancy. In fact, it may be as simple as preparing meals together, dining together, or sharing a moment with a few drinks by the fire. Danes put a high regard to this gathering since it strengthens their ties; it improves their relationships.

Of course, the Danes share the love for food, music, and dance with other countries. They are more than proud to share their unique dishes with visitors and take pride in maintaining healthy lifestyles.

They are also known for their love for drinking. In fact, they have one of the most liberal when it comes to alcohol consumption, with the legal drinking age in Denmark is pegged at 16 years old – a lot younger compared to those of other countries.

How the Danes spend their free time is also reflective of their fun-loving culture. The country is known to be home to an array of annual music festivals. Their love for music does not stick to a single genre, and the songs played range from rock, folk, to international rock.

Some of the biggest events include the Copenhagen Jazz Festival, the Folk Festival, the Skanderborg Festival, and the Roskilde Festival which is one of the biggest events in Europe. Aside from music and dance, they are also known to love a good laugh. They love to joke about life and its many ironies, and they joke about it a lot. This reflects their easy going nature.

Despite its strong ties with its heritage, Denmark is one of the most culturally progressive countries in the world. They were one of the first countries to embrace gender equality and social equality. As much as possible, they remain modest about how they live their lives because this helps them avoid judging others – an important component of building successful ties with people.

Thus, in the heart of all these situations lie the Danish love for socialization and strengthening their current relationships. They love eating and drinking, but more so when shared with the people they love.

Drinking and rocking out at festivals are fun because these moments create memories and connections. With this in mind, it becomes easier to understand hygge. With its varied translations to non-Danish speakers, it is safe to say that one of its definitions means having a good time with people who are close to their hearts.

3 - Work-Life Balance

Another factor to consider when trying to understand happiness and the Danish lifestyle is the way they spend their work and leisure time. Danes are hard-working individuals, but they also know how to have a good time. In fact, they're true masters of work-life balance.

Work-Life Balance is defined as the ability to successfully create a balance between attaining career-related goals and leisure time. This means choosing to enjoy one's free time instead of worrying about what lies ahead at work. In effect, those who are able to create this balance experience an improved quality of life. They begin to value their health and see that there is more to life than just earning money.

In Denmark, much of this stability is attributed to the working conditions generally offered to employees. Danes enjoy work flexibility. They are among the first nations to adopt a work-from-home scheme for their employees.

Additionally, they are also showered with various benefits which are necessary to ensure that they have enough time for leisurely purposes. This includes annual 5-week paid holidays, comprehensive maternity benefits, and other similar social welfare benefits.

In fact, the way they spend their lunch break tells the difference between Denmark and other countries. When Danish employees take their lunch, they make sure to leave work where it should be. They make use of their time to fully enjoy their meals and interact with their colleagues. As much as possible, they avoid talking about their work during this time and simply focus on what is happening at present.

However, this does not mean that those who are not provided with these benefits will never achieve this envied work-life balance. In fact, one doesn't even have to go to Denmark to work or have a Danish employer. It must be remembered that work-life balance does not depend on one absolute equation.

The different circumstances faced by different people contribute to how they prefer to spend their free time. Thus, it all boils down to a conscious choice of not allowing work to consume much of one's day. It means not being afraid of leaving unfinished paperwork once the shift is over. It means accepting that this is what the limited human capability can do, and that's perfectly okay.

4 - Happiest People In The World

Although they are extremely proud of their Viking heritage, the Danes are now a more peaceful bunch. Year after year since its inception in 2012, Denmark has consistently been in the top ranks of the World Happiness Report conducted by the United Nations.

In fact, it has held the top spot for the years 2013, 2014, and 2016. And in those times when they are holding the third or second spot, the difference between their happiness score with that of the first place is not significant.

A similar survey, the Eurobarometer, reflects the same statistics. This poll is regularly conducted by the European Commission, and since it began in 1973, Denmark has consistently been holding the top spot for the happiness survey. Thus, it can be concluded that indeed, the Danes are the happiest people on earth.

Where this happiness stems from is what makes it intriguing. Some people attribute it to the high value the government places on social welfare services. Although it is a known fact that the taxes in Denmark are relatively higher compared to other countries, much of the tax money redounds to the citizen's welfare.

Denmark has the most impressive healthcare systems where people enjoy free access not only to hospitals but also to medical procedures.

University students also benefit from perks such as monthly grants, in addition to free tuition fees, which are available to both graduate and undergraduate degrees. The average Danish work week is also composed of 37 hours, a few hours shorter than the average 40-hour workweek in most countries.

These are only among the many benefits that the government offers its citizens. Through these, it is undeniable that Danish people already feel a sense of security. They are assured that there will be a strong support system to lean on in the case of emergencies or temporary unemployment.

However, others also believe that this happiness does not depend on what the government offers its people. They relate it to an internal calmness and happiness that is innate in the Danish culture. This is reflected in the way they spend their free time. It can also be felt by the Danish sincerity when it comes to dealing with people. When all these factors come together, hygge is believed to be present.

Thus, what is truly at the core of living life the Danish way is not solely based on external factors. It greatly deals with internal factors and behavioral patterns which the Danes have grown accustomed to for years.

On a positive note, this means that it is possible to mimic this lifestyle even without going to Denmark to experience it firsthand. To fully embrace the lifestyle, one must begin with understanding the concept of hygge. This is where it gets tricky because hygge has many meanings to different people.

Hence, throughout this journey towards celebrating life the Danish way, one must keep in mind that hygge may mean all these things: a lifestyle focused on coziness, being aware of one's emotions, appreciating the simple things in life, embracing the present, and placing a high value on relationships.

Another key concept which goes hand-in-hand with hygge is jantelov. This is the natural law which is common in all Scandinavian countries. Jantelov was adopted as part of their culture in the early 1920s, and it teaches that life is to be lived modestly.

It discourages a person from parading his success in front of others. The concept of Jantelov discusses how being discreet about one's superiority or inferiority in terms of material wealth makes them happier individuals.

This is also the reason why Danes are also slow to judge others. When one judges another, the tendency is to fear being ridiculed or being considered as inferior. The tendency is to exhaust their bodies by working beyond what they can handle for the sake of obtaining material riches to brag about.

When they fear being judged, the tendency is to try to be perfect just to please others. Unfortunately, people-pleasing is a known cause of depression and burnout. It does not make a person happy at all.

Another factor to consider is how the Danes spend their money. In most countries, people see the abundance of money as a symbol of success and the lack of it as a source of humiliation. They tend to spend their money on acquiring luxury items they don't even need. They strongly hold on to the idea that a big house in a fancy neighborhood is a basic human need to attain happiness.

In contrast, Danish people spend their money for other purposes. They are greatly satisfied with the properties they own, as long as it allows them to comfortably live in the present. The tendency is to use their money as a means to enjoy life, like for the purpose of socializing with others.

Looking at all these concepts from a larger viewpoint, it is easy to see that the true evils are materialism and perfectionism. The Danes have mastered living a simple life which neither adheres nor believes in these ideals.

It helps them to enjoy what they have at present and just live in the moment. This quality helps them strengthen their bonds and be compassionate towards others. This is the true secret to their happiness.

However, keeping all these in mind seems like a lot to take in, especially for beginners. One may be tempted to revert back to his old lifestyle just because it is the easy way out. When that temptation takes over, consciously remind himself of his purpose for embarking on this journey: to live a life filled with happiness and contentment, just like the Danes.

5 - Simple Things

An Overview

A popular saying states that the greatest things in life are the simple things. And this statement couldn't be any truer. When people live simple lives, the tendency is to worry less, since the time he spends in thinking about his troubles is reduced. However, one can argue that this concept of simple living is merely a product of imagination which only exists in books.

Skeptics feel that simple living is an impossible feat to attain, especially considering life's many unexpected turns and challenges. They believe that life is meant to be lived lavishly with big, fat bank accounts in order to have a cushion when life takes a turn for the worse.

What most are unable to realize is that simple living doesn't mean completely letting go of a demanding career. Neither does it mean that a person should put off his dream of buying a big house. What it actually means is to live a life while cultivating thoughts of simplicity.

This means being aware of the simple things, and that these are the things that truly matter to make a person happy. Although it may manifest externally, it is more of an internal phenomenon. When that happens, both the mind and the heart becomes happy.

Of course, life's many events and challenges make appreciation of the simple things difficult. More often than not, these simple pleasures are often taken for granted. Although one has food on the plate, his mind is wandering elsewhere due to his obligations.

He may physically be with his family, but all he can ever think about is the workload he wasn't able to complete. Cultivating these thoughts prevent a person from enjoying the simple things because he is not living in the present.

Thus, a person must know how to control his thoughts in order to overcome these challenges. Reflection is the secret towards this goal. It means leading a full and conscious life by knowing at what stage you are in life right now, and being mindful of the present.

When this happens, a person is said to have found his inner peace. And when one lives with this state of calmness, he experiences psychological, physiological, and spiritual benefits. This includes developing self-confidence, concentration, improved memory, reduced anxiety, and a deeper understanding of oneself.

Hygge and Simplicity

One of the more popular definitions of hygge is that it is a state of coziness. Thus, one must be able to understand what this coziness really means. Contrary to popular belief, coziness does not mean sleeping in an expensively comfortable bedroom which is furnished with state-of-the-art facilities.

Coziness, in relation to the concept of hygge, actually means appreciating what one has at the moment and being happy with it. Thus, hygge is very much alive in a person who enjoys his simple bed and blanket compared to a person who has it all but is busy thinking of ways to obtain more.

In this scenario, the former is able to appreciate what he has at present, which the latter is unable to see. Thus, the former knows what it means to be cozy.

The Danes are experts at celebrating the simple things in life. After all, hygge is sometimes described as the cozy feeling one has whenever he highly regards the ordinary daily moments and considers them as more valuable than money.

5 - SIMPLE THINGS

More often than not, people allow themselves to be bogged down by this fast-paced world and their desire to be perfect all the time. In effect, they fail to stop and appreciate the simple things which, unknown to them, are the keys towards genuine happiness.

The Danish outlook towards appreciating the little things is believed to have something to do with the way they use their money. Generally, people prefer to spend money on life's many luxuries. They all want to have a big house, a brand new car, the most expensive pieces of jewelry, and other extravagant items.

They fell into the trap of believing that society will only consider them as worthy if they are successful, and that success is characterized by the amount of riches and properties owned.

In contrast, Danes prefer to use their money on interacting with others. Whether it is for a celebratory purpose, sharing hardships, or simply to share experiences, Danes love to be surrounded by people.

And when this happens, hygge is all around. It is present in the food they eat; it is in the way they share their stories.

And through the years of doing so, hygge has developed into a lifestyle and a national cultural treasure.

Thus, it is safe to say that socialization plays an important role in embracing the Danish way of life. When people socialize, they feel a sense of belonging. When they feel the warmth of being welcomed, it creates the positive feeling of being connected and appreciated.

This helps them see the bigger picture that they are not alone in this world. They start to realize that they can share their troubles and worries with their others, and when they do so, they feel better about themselves.

6 - The Role of Media

Of course, everyone deserves to live a comfortable life. But what most people don't know is that this can never be attained if worrying is in control of their lives. This task of letting go is not a walk in the park, especially with today's media bombarding everyone with misleading messages of materialism.

When the media shows these messages, the normal response is to want to be perfect. Their view of coziness or happiness is greatly distorted. This, in turn, cause people to work extremely hard to attain whatever the media tells them to obtain – whether it's a perfect body, the perfect car, or the perfect house – because they are made to believe that all these will make them happy.

This occurrence is rooted in the human desire to know the purpose of their existence. They often wonder why they are alive, and whether the universe has a specific purpose for him to achieve.

Sometimes, this curiosity ends up with him believing what the media shows him. When the images display a happy person enjoying his new car, he is inclined to buy a new car based on the belief that he will be happy.

However, people fail to realize that these media messages are often only a means to promote a product. Without a doubt, it leads to feeling a positive emotion which is often mistaken as happiness. One must remember that true happiness is long-term, while what they are experiencing is only temporary. In order to find this true happiness, the main goal must be to find the cause of happiness at a deeper level.

This path to self-discovery begins with asking oneself of the things which make him happy. Surprisingly, the answer to this assessment is not the material wealth of this world. They start to realize that it really is the simple things that matter to make life worth living.

It is being able to spend time with loved ones, eating a hearty meal, or drinking his favorite beverage. When a person allows himself to indulge in these little things, he starts to feel less stressed out.

In contrast, when people let their troubles take over their emotions, they make their world revolve around it. Once the temporary happiness brought about by these material luxuries begin to fade, they start to crave more of these luxuries. The tendency is to keep working hard to maintain that expensive lifestyle.

This makes him lose track of the present. He fails to appreciate the little things, and a continued adherence to this lifestyle eventually leads to burnout. And when that happens, they realize that they're not happy at all.

To contrast, when people take time off from their busy schedules, they start to feel a little less stressed out. This little pause has caused them to see that there is more to life than just working to pay the bills. Additionally, these seemingly insignificant pauses help them to think clearly once they resume with their work.

When they realize that this makes them feel good about themselves, they begin to include these breaks into their schedules. They make sure to allocate time to grab a book, catch a movie, or simply spend time with family and friends. And when this happens, they are subconsciously letting go of their worries.

Again, embracing this kind of lifestyle will not be a walk in the park. It will not be an overnight transformation. It demands a lot of time and requires a great deal of sacrifice. One must be willing, determined and patient to attain this goal.

7 - How To Embrace The Simple Things

Cultivating simplicity as a way of life effectively reduces a person's stress levels and anxiousness. He also lives life from a satisfied point of view which cannot be disturbed by any subliminal message promoting materialism. And with these benefits in store, it becomes easy to see why simple living is a key component of hygge.

Since hygge is an internal state, it is often associated with particular events which manifest it. It is not a specific activity that one has to follow based on what's written in the books. Its presence is felt when one shares his authenticity with others. It is there when he opens up his vulnerabilities, and accept other's vulnerabilities without judgment. In fact, even a simple conversation can display hygge.

To begin with embracing a life of simplicity, one must determine the things that make him happy. He should create an internal awareness of the things which he holds dear to his heart. He must learn to let go of the idea that happiness can be brought by money. Instead, he should open his eyes and heart to the things that money can't buy.

Perhaps the best illustration to this is time. For those who know how to value it, they know that time is a luxury. It is a fleeting concept, and whatever transpires in a certain moment only happens once. When one fails to appreciate it at a certain instance, he has lost that chance forever. It can neither be returned nor re-lived.

This is the reason why the Danes live in the moment. They fully understand how the concept of time works hand-in-hand with the appreciation of the simple things in order to be happy. They also understand that life is meant to be lived by creating an awareness of what is going on around him because it helps him react properly to his environment.

When people live by this lifestyle, it causes him to stop and smell the flowers or listen to the street musician. In effect, he realizes how life is meant to be lived – by taking a break once in a while and just be happy with what is going on around him.

As soon as they learn the art and beauty of this lifestyle, they start to feel better about themselves. And once they do, they start to see the world through a different perspective.

They look at life with a more positive outlook. They begin to face their fears and problems and solve them rationally.

Overall, life becomes a lot easier. He will start to feel care-free.

Remember, when people allow themselves to be turned down by everything that's happening around them, they overlook these little things. They allow worrying and stressing out over the things that they do not have control of to take over their lives.

8 - Practices and Activities

Learning to let go of a former lifestyle to embrace simplicity can be quite the challenge. It requires patience and continuous effort in order to materialize. Although difficult, it is definitely not impossible. Usually, it only needs reinforcement which is manifested in the physical world. Change must start at home.

This change can be as simple as decluttering the house. Minimalism is a relatively new concept which embraces the simple life. Like what its name implies, it encourages the minimal use of furniture.

It helps them appreciate and be comfortable with what they already have. This also helps them train their mind to see the beauty in simple things. Once the brain has become accustomed to it, it follows that it would be easier to welcome the new lifestyle.

Decorating the home with candles is also commonly associated with hygge. With hygge's origins in the dark winters of Scandinavia, the Danish ancestors often decorated the streets with candles to illuminate and give it life. Today, candles are still a great way to appreciate the simple things.

Some people use it as a symbol of hope, or as a reminder

that there will always be a way to illuminate the darkness. Others also take pleasure in the simple way it livens up a room, or how it fills the room with a relaxing aroma.

But perhaps the best aspect of simplicity practice is how one can change without spending anything. Simple things like going outside can greatly boost one's happiness meter, especially one done on a daily basis. The fresh air and the vitamin D is a bonus.

Others share how taking naps or listening to a good song can boost their moods and reduce their stress levels. There are also those who fall in love with the beauty of how the sun rises and sets. And the list goes on!

Oftentimes people get caught up in their jobs that they indeed fail to see the beauty of the simple things. They take it for granted and brush it aside as a normal occurrence which is necessary to live one's life.

Unfortunately, when they do these activities, they still focus on whatever's troubling them – their work, their numerous tasks, or chores. Although they're doing the little things, they're not really embracing the thought of it – which is exactly what they should be doing.

8 - PRACTICES AND ACTIVITIES

It is not a secret that simplicity is an attitude. Better yet, it is a learned attitude – and it's never too late or too early to start practicing it. However easy it may seem to begin this journey, it actually takes a lot more willpower.

An important piece of advice to remember is to be honest with oneself. Being honest with one's feelings and desires makes him realize what he really wants. Oftentimes, society shapes what people think they want. In reality, it is just an impossible standard which only leads to burnout. When one is aware of what makes him happy, it is only then that he can start working towards that happiness.

Unfortunately, it is not that easy. One may be faced with challenges such as the fear of not being good enough and worrying about being embarrassed. This makes him vulnerable, and this may even be enough to send him back to his old routine. The key to letting go of these negative feelings, as counterproductive as it may seem, is to embrace them.

When one learns to accept his vulnerabilities, he begins to love himself for who he really is. This helps him realize what he loves, what he hates, and what he wants to do with his life. It also helps him connect with others which, in turn, allows others to open up to him.

This makes him realize that he is not alone in facing his troubles. He starts to see the bigger picture that he is not alone in this world, and that there are others who are experiencing the same and that they are willing to help.

If these activities seem to be too overwhelming, there are also little day-to-day activities to try. The following are recommended activities which aim to help people consciously choose to see the simplicity in the things that surround them:

Breathe

Nothing makes a person feel more alive than breathing. When the day becomes demanding, it always helps to pause for a while and take deep breaths. Not only does it help a person get enough oxygen into the brain to reduce stress, but it is also a great reminder that life is more than just working for a living. Often, it even helps a person regain his focus when his tasks seem so challenging.

Listen to music

When people listen to music, the tendency is to completely allow himself to be engulfed by the beat. A few minutes into a song completely helps in letting go of anxieties to help a person relax. It is advised that he listen to music and completely let go of his other thoughts. Otherwise, his thoughts will take over, losing hold of the purpose of the activity.

Enjoy a meal

Eating or drinking are often taken for granted. Most of the time, people just eat because they need sustenance. What they don't know is that it is a great way to interact with others – whether they are family, friends, or work colleagues. This helps them build meaningful connections and help them appreciate the fact that they have food to eat for the day.

Grab a drink

Whether it is a cup of hot chocolate, tea, or an alcoholic beverage, a good drink is known to uplift a person's spirits. Of course, that is if he makes sure to enjoy it. Indulge and appreciate its flavor. Determine which flavors are good, or which one goes well with a certain snack.

Sing

It doesn't have to be perfectly in tune, and it doesn't have to be for anyone. Sing for yourself, and just because it makes you feel good. It also helps in letting go of one's inhibitions to help him show people how authentic he can be.

Watch a movie

Sometimes, all it takes to unwind after a stressful day is a good movie. What genre it falls under doesn't even matter. As long as it makes a person feel happy and more relaxed – even if it's the latest gruesome thrillers – then watch it, by all means.

Watch the sun set

One of the most beautiful natural phenomena is the sunset. With its many colors painting the sky, this breathtaking daily occurrence is nothing if not breathtaking. It tells a person that when the day ends, it takes all the stress away with it because a new day lies ahead.

Play with pets

A lot of pet owners can attest to how their pets effectively help them to let go of their worries. Pets are awesome creatures who will love his owner regardless of whatever his job is or whatever he is going through in life. They are experts at showing affection and in giving life to a dull room.

Read a book

Sometimes, a good book is all the company one needs. It is a great source of both knowledge and insight. It also helps people escape reality for a little while as they create their own universe as written based on its pages.

An important note when doing these activities is that one must be completely immersed in doing so. They must consciously choose to take a break and enjoy the moment as it is. Like the Danes, this also paves the way towards achieving that much-coveted work-life balance. Thus, one must be completely committed to it. Otherwise, these are all just pointless activities.

9 - Mindfulness

A key concept towards celebrating life the Danish way is mindfulness. Ordinarily defined, mindfulness is a way of paying attention to one's emotions and surroundings while being at the present moment. When one is aware of his internal and external experiences, these experiences help him cope with difficult situations. It helps them bounce back instead of sulking over whatever is lost.

Mindfulness works by keeping one's emotions and feelings in check. Since they are aware of what they are experiencing at a certain moment, they categorize it as either a positive or negative emotion. Once they feel that negative emotions are starting to build up, they consciously take steps to let go of these thoughts and focus on a more positive outlook.

However, this must not be mistaken for running away from problems. In fact, mindfulness encourages a person to face his troubles head on. When a person gets to face his stressors, he starts to realize that it is all just a normal part in the day of a human being. They see that what sets a happy person apart from the rest is the way they handle these stressors.

People may not realize it, but this is an important component of life because it is based on the belief that balancing out emotions is the key to finding true happiness. In order to fully embrace this concept, one must keep in mind that this internal awareness brings about various emotions, both positive and negative.

These emotions allow a person to be strong whenever he is facing hardships. He does not allow himself to be over-whelmed by all the negativity, or disillusioned by too much positivity. It seeks to create a balance.

Importance and Benefits

As previously discussed, being mindful helps a person re-cover from hardships. It helps people deal with problems instead of running away from them. Thus, it cannot be denied that being aware of one's internal and external states has its benefits.

Generally, the benefits of mindfulness manifest in a per-son's psychological state. For example, a person who has been constantly practicing mindfulness is known to have developed a deeper sense of focus.

Since practicing mindfulness causes a person to be aware of his surroundings and emotions at all times, it eventually develops the way he focuses on his tasks. Additionally, they also learn to suppress distracting information, to truly help them to focus on the task ahead.

Mindfulness also means getting rid of stressors or reduce the effects of stress. When people are mindful, they are aware of the things that make them happy. In effect, they become selective of the environment they're in. They also refuse to allow negativity from taking over their emotions. It works by remodeling how the brain reacts to stress.

An improved memory is also a known benefit of mindfulness. This is an aftereffect of being able to focus. When a person focuses and is aware of the task he is doing, there is a higher probability of its retention. And even if the memory is not as accurate, it still helps a person practice and develop his cognitive skills. This is owing to the fact that mindfulness strengthens neural connections.

Daydreaming is also effectively reduced. Although daydreaming is encouraged for children to encourage their creativity, it is already considered as a waste of time as adults. In fact, too much daydreaming can also lead to a twisted view of the facts, and can even lead to depression.

Whereas, when a person is able to focus, the amount of day-dreaming is effectively reduced. It makes him aware of reality and whatever is happening around him. Nonetheless, it does not affect a person's creativity since various expressions of art can be used to foster mindfulness.

Although being aware deals with a person's internal state, mindfulness also has an impact on a person's physical state. This is the reason why athletes often train with their mind and bodies. Not only does it help them to stay focused, it also improves their overall coordination.

Finally, being mindful helps a person become satisfied with his relationships. When one is aware of what causes his happiness, the tendency is to choose these positive emotions. And when a person is happy, it radiates and affects his surroundings. In effect, those around him also feel happy in his presence. Thus, improving and strengthening relationships.

Hygge and Mindfulness

When a person successfully cultivates mindfulness, he is one step closer to living a happy life. This is so because mindfulness helps him live in the present and not worry about whatever is not there. In effect, this helps reduce stress and avoid feeling anxious.

Similarly, the Danes are often described as a people who enjoy living in the moment. It seems that a big part of their culture makes them fully commit to the moment they are living in. If it means having a picnic with friends, then the activities to be done must revolve around the picnic.

No one should worry about work or school. They have to stay focused in the present. Thus, it cannot be denied that mindfulness is a key ingredient to understanding and experiencing hygge.

An advantage of the Danes over other nationalities is that have already been practicing mindfulness at an early age. This is why they do not have to worry about altering their thoughts to welcome these new concepts. Being mindful is already like common sense to them.

One must not be disheartened because of this. Mindfulness, much like happiness, is a highly learnable trait. If one has the determination and willingness to do it, then it is highly probable to learn to be mindful.

Mindfulness Meditation

With the many benefits stemming from developing a mindful lifestyle, the first question which comes to mind is how to achieve it. Fortunately, everyone can practice being mindful. It does not require a person to be of a certain age or to come from a specific social stratum. Additionally, the activities and exercises are generally easy to perform. The real challenge lies in the will to do them constantly.

What goes hand-in-hand with the concept of mindfulness is meditation. Meditation is defined as the process of transforming the mind through various techniques which develop an internal consciousness.

Unknown to some, there are actually different types of meditation practice, depending on what one wants to achieve. But for the purpose of developing a state of mindfulness, one must commit to mindfulness meditation.

Mindfulness meditation deals with developing one's concentration by focusing on whatever is present at the moment. It is generally divided into four sub-categories, namely: breathing meditation, body scan meditation, loving-kindness meditation, and observing-thought mediation.

Like what its name implies, breathing meditation helps a person concentrate by drawing his attention towards his breathing. This is perhaps the most common type of medication. By focusing on one's breathing, a person can recognize when his thoughts are starting to wander off. When this happens, it will be easier to let go of these thoughts and focus back on the breathing.

Body scan meditation, on the other hand, teaches a person to focus on a specific body part. This makes allows him to keep in touch with his body, and be able to feel each part from an internal state. In effect, it helps the person let go of repressed emotions, which why it is often confused with relaxation.

The loving-kindness meditation teaches a person to focus on one's heart and eventually extend it towards others. It seeks to nurture positive emotions, even when dealing with pressing situations. It also inspires a person to be compassionate towards himself.

Finally, the observing-though meditation deals with being aware of one's thoughts. Through this type of meditation, a person is able to recognize whether a thought is positive or negative. Nonetheless, he is trained to simply recognize the feelings associated with these thoughts, and not to get carried away.

However, with the many thoughts which keep popping up into someone's mind, meditating can be quite challenging. That is why it is important to remember that meditation is not a one-time thing. It requires constant practice and absolute devotion in order to be perfected. Some even seek out professional help to make sure they do it properly, and there's nothing wrong with that.

Aside from meditation, there are also small practices which can help a person with developing his mindfulness. It includes:

Improving one's posture. More than altering one's physical appearance, it actually has a deeper impact on one's psychological state. When a person consciously tries to improve the way he stands, he develops an awareness towards his body, which is similar to the effects of body scan practice. It also helps him develop his self-confidence.

Being observant. Mindfulness is about creating awareness of the present, and there is no better way to develop this than by being observant. He must be able to observe the various events which are taking place all around him. He must relate these observations to the emotions he feels, and be able to categorize them as either positive or negative.

Letting go of judgments. This goes hand in hand with being observant. When a person observes, it is inevitable for him to the good and the bad sides of the situation. However, in order to be mindful, he must be able to take all of it as it is. He must refrain from making any judgment. Only when he is able to do so can he be said to be truly mindful of his surroundings.

Being in control of one's thoughts. Being human means having random thoughts, and a sign of mental strength is being able to control these thoughts. However, this does not mean completely blocking off all unrelated ideas. It simply means having the strength to accept these random thoughts as part of human nature and to let it go without lingering on it too much.

Again, these activities require constant and conscious practice in order to develop mindfulness. The more time a person devotes towards practicing, the faster it will be for him to feel the beneficial effects of mindfulness. Of course, it does not have to be done strictly on a daily basis. However, one is encouraged to do so whenever he is given a chance.

Remember, every habit starts from conscious practicing. Eventually, that habit will form part of one's lifestyle. And when it becomes a lifestyle, these seemingly challenging activities will already be second nature.

10 - Connection

At the heart of happiness lies the human desire to build healthy relationships with others. Through these various relationships – whether with loved ones, close friends, colleagues, or strangers – one is able to feel loved and supported. In turn, a person feels an increased sense of self-worth. It makes them happy. And at the root of these relationships lie having meaningful connections.

Connection is defined as a form of energy or a bond between people. When two people are said to be connected, they feel a sense of belongingness. This causes them to no longer be afraid of sharing their weaknesses and fears. They no longer fear being judged by their peers, or by anyone for that matter.

What most don't know about these connections is how it how great its impact is in one's life. It does not just have an impact on one's health, but it has an effect on one's overall well-being. When people have a strong social support system, they are able to dodge certain diseases and conditions. It is also proven to reduce one's mental decline.

Digging deeper into this phenomenon, it can be inferred that the cause of one's improved well-being is attributable to his being able to express himself, having a shared support system, and being able to share his experiences. Thus, it is not hard to see why people with the strongest relationships are the happiest. This is another secret that the Danes have successfully mastered.

Danes are known to value their relationships. In fact, where people of most countries prefer to spend their money on material things, the Danes prefer to spend it on strengthening their relationships. They also place a high value on wellbeing rather than on success and status. Thus, it cannot be denied that they have discovered the secret to building genuine connections as a part of their lives.

Luckily, one doesn't have to be of Danish descent to be able to learn and build genuine connections. Human beings are social creatures by nature, after all. All one needs is to reconnect with that primal need for connection.

Understanding Connections

With the abundance of technology available in this modern age, it is easy to see why a lot of people mistake this for genuine connections. True enough, these social networks brings together old friends and allow them to share updates with each other about whatever is happening in their lives.

Messages over cellular networks also help people to keep in touch with each other. Unfortunately, this is simply being communicative, and not the connection which needs to be developed under this chapter.

To explain further, what people post on social media is only one side of their lives. He creates an image of himself he wants to portray, thus perfectly planning out what which sides he must show. He ends up highlighting only his achievements and strengths, while successfully hiding all his imperfections.

Oftentimes, one does not allow others to see the negative aspects of his life for fear of being ridiculed. In this sense, these digital communications may even hinder the development of healthy relationships.

This is not genuine connection. In order to cultivate this genuine connection, one must completely understand how compassion works. This compassion, in turn, can only be fulfilled when a person opens himself up others to see. This includes sharing his fears, weaknesses, and vulnerabilities.

However, before sharing his imperfections with others, he

must be able to accept who he is first. This helps him realize he is human, and part of being human is being imperfect. This makes him slow to judge others, and accept whatever judgment is thrown his way.

Once a person is able to embrace his imperfections, people will start to see him as an authentic human being. This authenticity draws people to him because they feel like they can also be themselves around him. When this happens, they begin to see that they are not alone in their journey.

They realize that there are others who also share their pain, and who are also experiencing the same troubles. They develop both self-compassion and compassion towards others. They begin to see life through the lens of positivity. Thus, they feel happy.

Benefits of Building Connections

Forging relationships with people and strengthening those which are already existing is one of the building blocks to living a happy life. It is also important to note the many benefits of building connections in order to appreciate it.

First of all, it increases a person's self-worth. Self-worth is defined as the value placed by the person onto himself.

When he is surrounded by people whom he loves and who loves him in return, he feels a sense of belongingness. When this happens, he begins to see himself as a human being capable of being loved. Thus, his self-worth increases.

Building connections also boosts confidence. As discussed, a stepping stone towards building connections is opening up one's vulnerabilities for others to see. This can be pretty terrifying. Once he sees that he can be accepted despite it all, he gains a better understanding of what it means to be human.

He begins to realize that it's okay to be imperfect because everyone is imperfect. He then learns to love himself, which is an important factor in boosting one's confidence.

It also teaches people to be compassionate. Much must be learned about compassion. Ordinarily understood, compassion is seen as being there for a person and listening to his troubles.

However, one can only be compassionate if he truly understands what the other person is going through, and to listen without judgment. Listening is easy, but to avoid giving judgment requires hard work. Thus, a key component to this is opening up of one's vulnerabilities is to help the other see and feel that he is not alone.

It inspires creativity. Being connected means opening up and embracing the many emotions which accompany it. These emotions inspire creativity since it helps a person express himself through various forms of art, like speech, writings, paintings, or dance.

Finally, it leads a person away from depression and other mental conditions. Sometimes, all a depressed person needs is someone to share his experiences with, and that the person will accept him without judgment.

When one is able to successfully build relationships with others, he knows that he is accepted for who he is. Since he has displayed his imperfections at the onset of their relationship, he knows that he was welcomed with open arms regardless of his human limitations.

When a person knows that he is loved regardless of these imperfections, he experiences positive feelings. However, when he learns to accept his imperfections – regardless of how people will react to it – he feels genuine happiness.

How to Connect with Oneself

What one should understand is that connection must begin with oneself. He must able to see his flaws and vulnerabilities and accept them as a part of who he is. Once he sees himself as an imperfect being and be okay with it, then he can open himself up to others.

In turn, he becomes compassionate. This helps him to open up to others. They begin to see his sincerity, and they open up as well. Fortunately, being compassionate is contagious.

The first step is to start with a mindset of connection. In order to do so, one must understand what building connections mean. He must realize that it is not just about knowing who a person is by name, neither does it mean being aware of what he likes, or what he dislikes. It means developing a deep bond with another to make relationships last.

Once there is already a clear idea of what being connected is, one must determine his own weaknesses. Since connecting with oneself is the stepping stone towards connecting with others, it is important to know his own vulnerabilities.

This is so because it makes a person relatable, and when he is relatable, people are more comfortable around him. This makes for a strong foundation. It also helps him become more sensitive about his reactions and when interacting with his surroundings.

Finally, one must learn what he wants. An integral part of the internalization process is discovering what he wants. In this way, he knows what keeps his emotions stable, and what he needs to do to stay positive. And when he exudes a positive character when dealing with others, the more they are attracted to him.

When all of these factors are put together, a person starts to appear more authentic to others. Authenticity is a quality which attracts like-minded people. It is the stepping stone towards compassion – an important aspect to connecting with others.

How to Connect With Others

Once a person learns to connect with himself, only then can he be ready to connect with others on a deeper level. In order to do so, he must learn how to be compassionate – both to himself and towards others.

Compassion is at the heart of connecting with others since it offers a genuine sense of acceptance. Generally defined, compassion refers to understanding the circumstances experienced by a person without providing any form of judgment. It means more than listening or offering pieces of advice. It means being there in that moment, and to genuinely empathize with the person.

However, understanding how compassion works can be tricky. It is often misunderstood as listening to a person's troubles and telling him what he wants to hear. Or worse is to put the blame on someone else. This should not be the case.

True compassion lies in not being afraid of sharing similar experiences with the other. It helps a person to see the bigger picture that he is not the only one who is living an imperfect life. Being compassionate means helping the other open up about his problems and just be there to listen without judgment. It means genuinely being there for others.

Connection Practice

Among the many components of hygge, cultivating connections seem to be the trickiest. It requires several elements prior to being completely imbibed as a way of life. Nonetheless, healthy relationships are not created overnight. The following are suggested activities to help a person develop and practice being connected with people:

Talk to people. The most basic activity in order to develop connections is to actually talk to people. Try to learn more about them by listening to the things they love to do or what they want to be, and try to avoid making any comment or judgment. This helps develop compassion by trying to understand the circumstances of a person which are directly linked to his desires.

Express gratitude whenever possible. Being grateful for what one has not only makes a person grateful but also makes him realize that he has more than he needs in this life. His life may not be perfect, but he has what he needs to survive – and that's more than enough.

Be kind to others. Being kind to others is, undeniably, an element of compassion. Being kind doesn't mean trying hard to be a friend in an instant. Sometimes, it can be as simple as smiling at a person who has had a rough day.

Extend a helping hand. Again, an element of compassion. When someone is experiencing troubles, they have the tendency to focus on their worries. They start to think that they are failures and no one wants to associate with them.

Extending a helping hand can instantly change this mindset. Once they realize that they have a support system to back them up, they not only feel positive about themselves, but they also get a much-needed confidence boost.

Ask for help is also a great way to develop connections. This shows people that one has acknowledged that he cannot be successful if he does things on his own. It is a sign of acknowledging weaknesses, and it makes people realize that it's okay to be weak sometimes.

Choose to do one's passions. When one works on what he is passionate about, the tendency is for people to be drawn to him. In today's society, a lot of people is being discouraged from chasing their passions because it doesn't earn much.

However, when a person chooses to do what he is passionate about − whether as a career or not − he reflects happiness and authenticity. As previously mentioned, people are drawn to authentic personalities.

And finally, live in the present. Much of the Danish lifestyle deals with living in the moment, and this is also true when strengthening or building connections. When people live in the moment, the tendency is to let go of whatever wrongs have happened in the past. They focus on the positive emotions of the present and choose to live with it.

11 - Conclusion

True enough, the Danes live their lives differently. They tend to live it from an optimistic point of view and make sure to bask in the glory of the moment. The way they see materialism and perfectionism also vary from how the rest of the world views it.

In fact, money is spent differently in Denmark. They do not put material wealth on a pedestal. Instead, they make sure to spend it on the things that truly matter – the simple things in life.

Once a person sees the difference between the Danish lifestyle and his own, it becomes easy to understand why they are consistently dubbed as the happiest people on earth. Of course, this doesn't mean that the Danes do not worry about anything at all. Because the truth is, they do.

All human beings are wired to feel all these emotions, and the Danes are definitely not immune to feeling them. The secret lies in how they allow themselves to react to these stressful situations.

Much of this secret lies on the Danish concept of hygge. Hygge, as discussed, does not have a specific English translation. However, it has much to do with the many positive emotions which go hand in hand with the lifestyle of coziness. Sometimes, it is also used to describe the special quality of happiness one feels when he allows himself to appreciate the simple things, and by making sure to live in the moment.

Clearly, then, hygge does not only depict a single scenario. It is actually composed of various components such as mindfulness, connection, and appreciation of the simple things.

Mindfulness, as an element of hygge, deals with a person's internal awareness. When a person is in check with his emotions, it helps him to react appropriately to his surroundings. In effect, this helps him be aware of the many emotions he is feeling, and to effectively categorize them as either good or bad.

This is important to understanding the concept of hygge because it gives a person with the ability to bounce back after experiencing hardships. It is also important to note that mindfulness effectively reduces a person's stress levels by not allowing himself to be drowned in its negativity.

Another key component, and perhaps the trickiest, is connection. Connection is responsible for how a person deals with another. On a deeper level, it is the true source of healthy and happy relationships. And as observed, the Danish people highly value their relationships as shown by their love for socialization.

But, although human beings are naturally social beings, it takes more than being able to talk and listen to genuinely connect with others. In order to experience this level of connection, it is important for a person to cultivate compassion first.

Compassion, as an element of connection, not only refers to empathy. It deals with both being self-compassionate and being compassionate towards others. In order to be self-compassionate, one must learn to accept his vulnerabilities as part of being an imperfect human being.

He must take judgments and criticisms head on and not be bothered by them at all. On the other hand, being compassionate towards others means not being afraid to share his own troubles to help the other see that he is not the only one suffering. When a person has successfully cultivated compassion, forming connections will already be second nature to him.

Another important component of hygge is appreciating the simple things. Oftentimes, these simple things are so interconnected with how one lives his life that he takes them for granted.

When he is overwhelmed by his troubles and fears, the tendency is to focus on these fears. He becomes too distracted to realize how delicious his meal is, or how beautiful the sunset looks. And when that happens, the tendency is to be drowned in all the negativity.

Luckily, when one focuses on the simple things, he realizes that it is all it takes to live. He learns to stop and focus on what he has at the moment, knowing that it is all that he needs in that very moment. He becomes thankful that he is still alive and breathing. He realizes that although he does not have a lot, he knows that what he has is enough.

These are the main components that are generally associated with hygge. Nonetheless, embracing the Danish lifestyle also means understanding why they were wired to behave that way. People are quick to point out the fact that the Danes have perfected the art of work-life balance. This lies in the way they spend their leisure time.

With all these important elements and concepts in mind, it will be easier for any person to mimic the Danish lifestyle without traveling thousands of miles. In fact, one does not even have to spend any money in order to fully embrace this lifestyle. This is owing to the fact that all of these are behavioral patterns which can be learned.

However, re-training the brain can be mentally exhausting. It would inevitably demand a lot of time for practice and would require a lot of willpower. One must knowingly choose to practice each of these components, and that can be physically draining.

Sometimes, the temptation to quit can become too overpowering. And that is why it is important to remember that this journey will not be easy. He must keep his eyes focused on the prize. Eventually, and without even knowing it, he is finally able to celebrate life the Danish way.

Book 2 - Hygge 02

Eliminate Stress With The Rules of Hygge (Denmark, Nordic Theory, Celebration of Life, Healthy, Positive Living)

1 - Introduction

I want to thank you and congratulate you for downloading the book, "Hygge Book 2: Eliminate Stress With The Rules of Hygge (Denmark, Nordic Theory, Celebration of Life, Healthy, Positive Living".

We live in a modern world that's filled with pressure and demands, so it's no wonder why stress is already a part of our daily life.

A small amount of stress is good because it pushes you to do the things that need to be done. It enables you to face your problems head on and find workable solutions. A little stress inspires you to take on the path of excellence. However, too much of it is not good for you. In fact, it could kill you.

Stress can wreak havoc in your life. It could negatively affect your health and could lead to various health issues such as depression, anxiety, and auto-immune diseases.

Stress can also lead to mental deterioration. It can slow down your cognitive ability and can also negatively affect your career. When you're stressed out, you tend to be irritable and moody all the time. You may have a wild anger outburst at the slightest provocation and this could alienate you from your loved ones and possibly destroy your relationships at work and home.

People from all over the world are having a hard time dealing with stress. But, Danish people seem to have mastered the art of beating stress. Denmark is literally one of the darkest countries in the world. It is located in the Northern part of Europe, so it is cold, gloomy, and dark most of the time.

Denmark also collects the highest taxes in the world. But, despite this, Denmark is still one of the happiest countries in the world. In fact, it was hailed as the happiest country in 2014 and 2015. So, what's their secret? It's the ritual that's spelled as H-Y-G-G-E, but pronounced as Hoo-gah.

Hygge is trending online lately and is becoming the new buzzword among people who want to beat stress and live a more authentic life.

So, if you're stressed, burnt out and anxious all the time, it is high time that you learn the art of hygge. In this book, you'll learn how to decorate and organize your home to reduce stress and anxiety.

You'll also learn practical Danish techniques that can help

you relax after a long day at work. In this book, you'll also find useful self-care tips that can strengthen your mind and body connection and make you feel good about yourself and your life in general.

This book contains tips and workable strategies that will help you beat stress and improve the quality of your life.

It is time to take control of your stress before it controls you. Hygge is the well-kept Danish secret to happiness. If it worked for the Danes, it can certainly work for you, too.

Thanks again for buying this book, I hope you enjoy it!

2 - Hygge: The Secret of the Happiest Country in The World

Denmark is known as the home of Legos and the little mermaid. They are also known for their delicious beer brands such as Tuborg and Carlsberg. It is one of the most beautiful countries in the world and is considered a paradise for beach lovers and foodies.

But, Denmark is not all about sunshine and beautiful things. Its climate from May to August is pleasant. But the country experiences frequent snowstorms during the winter time. Despite the cold weather that can often leave people depressed, Denmark is considered as one of the happiest countries in the world. In fact, it was named as the happiest country in 2013, 2014, and 2015.

What is the secret to Denmark's happiness? Well, it's a mix of a few cultural, economic, and lifestyle factors. For one, Denmark has the lowest income inequality in the world. This means that there's not much difference between the income of the rich and the poor.

It also has one of the highest standards of living all over the world. They have a wide array of free public services such as education and medical services. The country also provides a high level of social security to its citizens. Education is free at all levels. The Danish government is also considered as the least corrupt government in the world.

Denmark is a great country with a thriving economy and an honest government. But, the real key to the happiness of the Danish people is a concept called Hygge (pronounced as Hoogah). Hygge has no English equivalent, but it is quite similar to coziness.

3 - Principles and Rules of Hygge

We will discuss these principles and their stress reduction effect later on in this book. To give you a clear picture of what this Danish lifestyle concept is, here's a list of the basic rules and principles of hygge:

Number One: Create A Cozy Atmosphere

Who doesn't want to live in a cozy home, right? But, most people spend a lot of time at work, at malls, or restaurants. When they're finally home, they're either watching TV or on Facebook. There's no wonder why less and fewer people pay attention to their homes.

But, your home is your personal space. It is your sanctuary and whether you like it or not, it is a part of you. So, you have to make sure that it is cozy and comfortable. Invest time, effort, and money in making your home beautiful and pleasing to the eye. This way, you'll feel relaxed when you go home from work.

Number Two: Live in The Present Moment

Living in the past makes you feel depressed and focusing on

the future causes anxiety. If you want to live a happy life, you have to live in the present moment.

Mindfulness has a lot of benefits. For one, it can relieve stress. Living in the present moment allows your body to adopt a more relaxed response to stress. It improves your health and reduces the symptoms of many diseases such as depression, heart disease, chronic pain, insomnia, and gastrointestinal difficulties.

A number of studies also show that mindfulness can alleviate anxiety disorders and eating disorders. It can even help cure substance abuse and can improve relationships.

When you live in the present moment, you get to appreciate the little things in life. You are grounded because you are fully awake and in touch with the reality. You are also more in control of your cravings, emotions, and body sensations.

Number Three: Practice Gratitude

Gratitude is one of the most powerful keys to happiness. According to a study published in the British Journal of Social Psychology, gratitude increases one's life satisfaction, happiness, vitality, and optimism. It instills forgiveness and reduces materialism. It also prevents the development of depression, anxiety, and other mental disorders.

Gratitude increases your confidence because when you appreciate yourself and what you have, you'll realize that you're blessed, valuable, and you have a lot to offer to the world.

Number Four: Live A Drama-Free Life

The Danes may look cold and reserved, but they are definitely drama-free. They avoid unhealthy relationships and establish healthy ones. They communicate clearly and honestly so the people that they love do not have to read between the lines.

They also have a habit of minding their own business. They do not give unsolicited advice and do not have a hard time saying no to requests that they are not comfortable with. They also avoid gossip whenever they can.

Number Five: Enjoy Life's Simple Pleasures

Hygge is all about creating a happy life and to do this, you have to enjoy life's simple pleasures like popping a bubble wrap and holding hands with your loved ones. You can also enjoy a good workout.

Take time to enjoy the sunset or simply watch the children giggle and play. Have a good laugh with your friends and take a long bubble bath after a long day at work. You can simply place lemon slices in your water or iced tea.

Number Six: Create and Share Wonderful Memories with Your Loved Ones

Hygge is a modern lifestyle technique that you can use to achieve bliss. It is all about enjoying life and making the most out of it. So, if you are stressed out all the time, it's time to slow down, grab a cup of hot chocolate, chill, and practice the wonderful Danish art of living a happy life.

Number Seven: Be Yourself

The Danes understand that pretending to be someone you're not can backfire. It can push you beyond your limits and this could inevitably make you crash and burn.

Pretending to be someone that you're not will not make you happy. In fact, it will make you miserable and lose a sense of who you really are. Pretending to be someone is extremely exhausting and could take up a lot of your time and energy.

To practice Hygge, you have to embrace who you are and be comfortable with being yourself. You have to believe that who you are is enough and you do not have to pretend to be someone else just to win other people's attention.

People who cannot accept you for who you really are do not deserve to stay in your life. You have to believe that you are good enough. You are okay. Be honest about who you are and be open about your thoughts and feelings.

You are not perfect, but who is? You have to embrace your flaws and celebrate yourself – imperfections and all.

Number Eight: Be Independent, But Embrace Togetherness

The Danes believe in the power of independence. They believe that people who are independent are the only ones who can truly create an authentic relationship that's based only on love. But, they also realize the importance of being connected with other people. They know how essential togetherness is in building a happy life.

To live a fulfilling life, you have to establish rituals and traditions with the people you care about. You can have dinner with them every Sunday or go to the beach together during holidays.

Number Nine: Avoid Conflicts and Controversy

Conflicts and arguments are stressful. So, try your best to avoid arguments whenever you can. This does not mean that you have to roll over and let people walk over you. But, you have to do it in a peaceful manner. Avoid drama at all cost.

Try your best to stay away from conversations that may lead to a heated debate. Do not discuss religion or politics during dinner, parties, or events. Keep your conversations positive and inspiring. Do not brag or complain. Remember that your time is limited and each interaction you have with other people is an opportunity to inspire and them happy.

Number Ten: Take A Break Often

Your time in this world is limited and you do not want to spend it all at work. You have to balance work with pleasure. To enjoy a happy life, you have to take a break whenever you can.

Take a vacation and go to places you've never been to for at least once a year. You can go to Tokyo, Bangkok, or the beautiful island of Maldives. You can also take a trip to nearby beaches at least once a month just to unwind, shake the stress off, and enjoy.

Number Eleven: Take A Step Back and Clear Your Head

Life is filled with pressure and stress. So, when you're faced with deadlines and hundreds of tasks, take a step back and clear your head. You can do this by taking a walk in a park or meditating. The internet is also filled with virtual noise so you may want to skip looking at your social media accounts.

Hygge is not just about getting cozy. It is about taking care of yourself. Loving yourself and taking care of your mental and physical health are the most powerful keys to happiness. The Danes understand this, so it's no wonder that Denmark is one of the happiest countries in the world.

4 - Avoiding Messy Relationships: The Nordic Theory Of Love and Individualism

Too much stress at work can harm your relationships. But, being in the wrong kind of relationship is also a common source of stress. The Danes understand this and so they practice what the Scandinavians call the Nordic Theory of Love.

Before we discuss this theory in detail, let's take a step back and learn more about the Nordic countries. For those who are not living in Europe, the Nordic region is located in Northern Europe. It includes the Scandinavian kingdoms of Sweden, Norway, and Denmark.

It also includes Finland, Iceland, Greenland, the Aland Islands, and the Faroe Islands. It also includes the beautiful cities and destinations such as Copenhagen, Reykjavik, Stockholm, Turku, Bergen, Aarhus, Gothenburg, Stockholm, Oslo, Gotland, Jostedalsbreen, Laponia, Nordkapp, Mývatn, Nuuksio National Park, Stevns Cliff, Saariselkä, Sydfynske Øhav, and Þingvellir National Park.

Nordic countries are stunning and breathtaking. The region

is the home of the magnificent natural light show – Aurora Borealis. It is also the home of the wonderful and marvelous tourist destinations such as the Kirkenes Snow Hotel in Norway, Lapland, The Troll Wall, Hoyvika Beach, Stockholm, Lofoten, and the picture perfect city of Copenhagen in Denmark.

Nordics are known for their bright blue eyes and blonde hair. The Nordics are generally reserved. They do not make the first move or initiate conversations. They can be stoic but once you engage them in an interesting exchange of ideas, you'd find out that they are open-minded and friendly.

Most people view our relationships as part of our being. We are constantly looking for that one person to "complete us". We think that our happiness is tied with our friends or with the people we love.

The Nordics, including the Danes, think differently. They believe that "authentic love and friendship are only possible between people who are independent and equal". This may sound a lot like the concept of American individualism, but it's not. In her book "The Nordic Theory of Everything",

4 - AVOIDING MESSY RELATIONSHIPS: THE NORDIC THEORY OF LOVE AND INDIVIDUALISM

Finnish writer Anu Partanen discussed what she called "The Nordic Theory of Love."

She explained that when two people are independent and self-reliant, they are able to form a loving and healthy relationship. Although she discussed a number of other issues in her book such the health care system and the economic and social infrastructures in Northern Europe, the "Nordic Theory of Love" boils down to one thing - love is rooted in individualism and independence and not on dependence.

You see, most of us associate love with dependency. But, dependency is actually the central problem in most relationships and it can lead to a lot of stress. When you are dependent on the people that you love, you'd probably engage with people-pleasing behavior. You'll have a hard time saying "no" to requests that you're not comfortable with and you'll end up spreading yourself too thin.

When you depend on the people around you, you'll have poor boundaries. You feel responsible for other people's problems or feelings. You put other people's needs and wants above yours. You also have a strong need for control. Co-dependency can take a toll on your mental, emotional, and even physical health.

So, to avoid stress in your relationships, here's how you can apply the Nordic Theory of Love in your life:

Number 1: Stop Your People-Pleasing Behavior

You have to stop letting others define your self-worth. If people do not like you, well, that's not your problem. It doesn't make you less of a person. You are not going to be everyone's cup of tea, and that's okay. No matter what you do and how hard you try, there will always be a group of people who will not like you.

So, if you want to live a happy life, you have to stop bending over backward just to make people like you. You have to make peace with the fact that no matter what you do, not everyone is going to like you. So, stop trying to win everyone's affection.

You have to realize that you are just as important as other people. Stay away from people who are trying to manipulate and abuse you. Run away from people who try to exploit your kindness.

Remember, your value does not depend on other people's approval. You shape your own value by practicing self-love and self-respect. When you love and respect yourself, you have high self-esteem and you will not allow other people to take advantage of you.

To stop your people-pleasing behavior, you have to be assertive. Don't say "yes" when you mean no. Don't feel guilty about prioritizing your needs. Learn how to love yourself. You have to look after your own needs and work on your insecurities.

Number 2: Set Personal Boundaries

Do you always feel like people are taking advantage of you? Do you like saving people from their problems? Do you attract highly charged and toxic romantic relationships? Do you easily fall for someone? Do you have dramatic relationships? Do you have a hard time making a decision about your life? Do you feel guilty whenever you say no?

Do you feel like others are not showing you respect? Do you often worry about what others think about you? Do you feel that everyone is walking over you? If you answer yes to any of these questions, you may need to set healthy personal boundaries.

Setting personal boundaries is not easy, especially if you're a people-pleaser all your life. But, creating a personal boundary can do wonders in your life. It allows you to build healthy and mutually respectful relationships. It is also the true measure of your self-worth and self-esteem. If you have a healthy boundary, you'll develop self-respect and as a result, people will value and respect you.

To create personal boundaries, you have to be clear as to what is acceptable and unacceptable to you. Do you want your work mates to stop calling you after office hours? Do you want your partner to stop flirting with other people? Do you want your mom to stop meddling with your personal life? Do you want your friends to treat you with respect and stop making jokes at your expense?

Well, then, you need to be clear about your boundaries and call out people who habitually cross them. If your colleague is always late, call him out. If your mom is constantly criticizing your life decisions, then respectfully tell her that you are on top of your life and that you'd appreciate it if she stops meddling in your personal affairs.

If the people in your life choose not to honor your boundaries, then you should minimize contact with them or walk away from them for good.

Also, you need to stop fixing people. A lot of people try to fix other people's problems to win their love, affection, and attention. But, trying to fix other people is a complete waste of energy and time.

You have to learn to respect the people around you and recognize that they have all the skills and resources needed to solve their own problems. When you try to help other people all the time, you keep them from growing and learning new things.

Stop projecting your fears and dreams onto other people and start to separate yourself from others.

Number 3: Take Care of Yourself and Your Needs

Self-love is the center of both Hygge and the Nordic concept of love. To live a drama-free life, you have to love and take care of yourself. Remember that you cannot give what you do not have. When you take care of your own needs, you do not have to depend on others. You are completely self-reliant and so, you enter into relationships out of pure love and not out of desperation or need.

To avoid stress from dramatic relationships, you have to organize every area of your life. You have to take care of your finances and be on top of your business or career.

You have to eat healthy foods and drink clean water each day. Being healthy does not only ward off stress, but it also gives you the energy to spend time with your loved ones and grow your relationships.

Number 4: Let Go of Your Expectations

Our loved ones disappoint us all the time. In order to avoid relationship stress and practice the Nordic principle of love, you have to let go of your expectations and accept people for who they really are.

As human beings, our greatest need is to be accepted and loved for who we really are. So, try to be more understanding and accepting.

Number 5: Come As You Are

As mentioned earlier in the book, one of the key values of hygge is authenticity. To attract loving and mutually respectful relationships, you have to be yourself. You are lovable just as you are. Stop pretending to be someone else just to win the affection of the people you love. You are enough and you are special, just as you are.

Do not be afraid to be yourself and be vulnerable. Be honest about how you feel and avoid comparing yourself to others. Also, don't be afraid to stick to your personal values and beliefs.

Number 6: Spend Time With Your Loved Ones

The Nordics, including the Danes, celebrate individualism. But, they also encourage togetherness. They are reserved but are loving and affectionate to the people they care about.

To build authentic and loving relationships, you have to spend more time with your loved ones. No matter how busy your day is, take the time to share at least one meal each day with a person you love – it could be your spouse, your children, siblings, friends, or parents.

Take time to listen to their concerns and problems. Share jokes and laugh with them. Pay attention to their interests and passions. Always let them know that you care.

The Nordics know when to connect and when to disconnect. Their relationships are not perfect, but they are definitely drama-free.

Number 7: Avoid Toxic People

The world is filled with kind and loving people. But, every now and then, you'll meet toxic people. These people do nothing but complain and bring people down just because they are unhappy with their lives. They are manipulative, judgmental, and inconsistent. They act like you are not good enough. They are not supportive and caring. They like to argue and lie.

These people can drain all your energy. They manipulate, abuse, and take advantage of you. So, to live a drama-free life, stay away from them or try your best to limit your contact with them.

To live a drama-free life, surround yourself with loving
people who support your dreams. Be with people who accept you for who you are and who will be there for you no
matter what.

Take care of yourself so you won't have to depend on
someone else. But, stay connected to those who truly care
for you. You deserve mutually loving and respectful relationships that can help you deal with the difficulties in life.

5 - The Art of Getting Cozy

The Danes are not lazy. They just understand that work is not everything. They know that to maintain a happy life, one must achieve work-life balance. This is the reason why they have mastered the art of coziness or hygge.

The Danes are obsessed with interior design because they treat their homes as their "hygge headquarters". To master the art of coziness, you must slow down and enjoy the little things. You must also make your house livable, if not breathtakingly beautiful.

Get A Massage

Who doesn't want a good massage? Massage has an intense stress reduction effect. It also helps you deal with a number of health and medical issues such as headaches, insomnia, digestive disorders, sports injuries, and digestive disorders. It also helps treat the symptoms of anxiety and depression.

If you've been working too hard lately, reward yourself and get a good massage. You can try various types of massage such as deep massage, Swedish massage, trigger point massage, and sports massage.

You do not have to spend a lot of money to get a good massage. You can ask your partner to massage you. You can also do self-massage and massage your feet, arms, and shoulders.

Get A Good Night Sleep and Stay in Bed Whenever You Can

Most of the Danes are doing well financially. In fact, Denmark is one of the most stable economies in the world. But, they are not obsessed with their work. They are not sleep-deprived. They understand that to perform well at work and in life, they have to get enough sleep each night.

So make sure that you sleep 6 to 8 hours per night. Spray some lavender room mist. This can help improve your sleep quality. During weekends, stay in bed as long as you can. You've been working hard all week so give yourself a break and sleep longer during weekends.

Enjoy A Cup of Hot Chocolate or Tea

Warm drinks are comforting. They improve your digestion and detoxify your body. They improve blood circulation, slow down aging, and help you lose weight.

If you are feeling down or stressed out, whip a cup of hot

chocolate. This would help you to instantly feel good. If you try to avoid sugar, drink a cup of hot tea instead.

Sit By the Window and Read A Good Book

Reading a feel good book can help relax your entire body. If you are feeling stressed, sit by the window and read a good book. This will help you forget about your problems and worries. It will also stir your imagination and stimulate your mind.

Bake and Eat Cinnamon Bread

The Danes love cinnamon bread. What's not to like? Cinnamon bread is delicious and is packed with nutrients, too. Its main ingredient, cinnamon, can reduce blood pressure and lower your blood cholesterol levels.

It raises the HDL or good cholesterol and has strong anti-fungal and antibacterial properties. A number of studies show that cinnamon has anti-carcinogenic properties that help protect you from cancer. Amazing, right?

Drink Fruit Water

If you are not a fan of water, you can drink fruit water instead. Fruit water helps relieve stress and improves your mood. It detoxifies your body and strengthens your immune system, too.

But, where do you buy this fruit water? Well, you don't have to. You simply make it. Just mix cold water with sliced fruits such as orange, tangerine, strawberries, watermelon, and blueberries. You can also add herbs such as mint, rosemary, ginger, and cinnamon.

Declutter Your Home and Fill It With Beautiful Things

Your house is your personal space. So, it has to be clutter free. To live a comfortable and stress-free life, take time to clean and organize every room in your house. You have to clean your home twice or thrice a week. You also have to take time to organize your things at least once a month.

The Danes have mastered the art of maintaining a beautiful home. Copenhagen is one of the most beautiful cities in the world because of the beautiful buildings, amazing interiors, clutter- free streets, and cozy homes. Here are some of the tips that you can use to ensure that your house is beautiful, cozy, and clutter free:

Tip #1 – Purge Your House Often

Throw or give away the stuff that you no longer use. Keeping a lot of stuff in your house can cause overcrowding and this could lead to stress.

Check your refrigerator and throw out all the rotten food items. Organize your kitchen cabinets and place similar things together. For example, place all the spoons and forks in one drawer and place all the cup in one area. This will make it easier for you to look for things later on. Keep your kitchen squeaky clean all the time.

Get rid of the clothes that don't fit anymore. You can donate them to homeless shelters. When you're purging your house, you also need to get rid of things that you no longer use such as old receipts, old magazines, books that you no longer want, expired vitamins and medicines, expired makeup and perfume, and notebooks.

Maintaining a clean and clutter-free house can clear your mind and reduce stress. Plus, who doesn't want to live in a neat house?

Tip #2 – Invest in Beautiful Throw Pillows

Throw pillows are attractive and they keep you comfortable, too. To maintain a cozy home, invest in good throw pillows. Throw pillows are not only decorative, but they should also add comfort to your sofa. Choose throw pillows that are big, fluffy, soft, and stylish. You can cover them with colorful and soft pillow cases for added aesthetic value and comfort.

Tip #3 - Pay Attention to Curtains

Curtains are decorative and they create a certain ambiance in your home. So, it is important to choose high-quality curtains that blend well with the design and vibe of your home. If you want your home to feel warm and sunny during winter days, use colorful floral curtains. You can also use silky gold curtains with elaborate tassels if you want your home to feel like a palace or a Victorian mansion.

Tip #4 – Place A Fluffy Doormat On Your Doorstep

You want your home to be warm and welcoming. You can put a fluffy doormat outside your front door that says "Welcome to Our Cozy Home". This will make your guests feel welcome.

Tip #5 – Turn Your Bathroom Into a Spa

You do not have to spend hundreds of dollars in a spa. You can turn your bathroom into a spa. All you need to do is place river rocks around your bathroom. You can also fill your bath with aromatic essential oils.

Tip #6 – Use High-Quality Comforters

Comforters make your bed more cozy and warm, especially during winter time. To practice hygge, use high-quality comforters that fit into the design and colors of your bedroom. Choose light, fluffy, breathable, and warm comforters to maximize the coziness of your bed.

Tip #7 – Use a lot of candles

Scented candles are not only visually stimulating, but they

are also extremely relaxing. They create a warm glow in your home and they are stylish, too.

The Danes love candles. They place beautiful scented candles all around their homes to create a warm and cozier ambiance. You can do this at your own house as well.

Best-scented candles that you can use for your home

- Vanilla – This has a soothing scent and is a natural aphrodisiac. It provides a strong sense of satisfaction and comfort.

- Eucalyptus – This has strong healing and stress-reduction effects. It smells festive. Lighting Eucalyptus around your house makes you feel like it's Christmas all year long.

- Lavender – This candle has a calming scent. It has a peaceful, feminine, and tranquil scent, and helps relax every cell in your body.

- Apple Cinnamon - This candle has a sweet scent that, well, smells like apple cinnamon. It is extremely relaxing.

- Ylang Ylang Scented Candle – This candle has a sweet scent that helps reduce stress. It is a potent aphrodisiac, too.

You can use regular-shaped candles all around your house or you can use star-shaped or heart-shaped candles. You can find a lot of novelty candles at your favorite home centers.

Using candles is fun and it can release stress. But, let's face it. It can be dangerous at times.

Candle safety tips

- Do not place the candles near anything that can easily catch fire like drapes, carpets, bedding, books, and flammable home decor.

- Place the candles in stable candle holders.

- Always use candle holders.

- Place the candles in a well-ventilated room.

- Do not burn the candles all the way down to the holder.

- Do not extinguish the flame using water, especially if you are using a glass candle holder.

- Do not use a candle as night light.

- Do not leave the candle unattended.

- Make sure that each candle is at least four inches apart.

It's good to keep your home warm and cozy, but you have to put the safety of your family first.

Tip #7 – Use Fluffy and Soft Rugs

Fluffy rugs make your home look more elegant. They are gorgeous and they give your feet that comfy tingly feel.

Tip #8 – Buy a Netted Canopy Bed

A netted canopy bed can make you feel like a royalty. So, if you want to feel like a queen or a king, then it's a good idea to spend a few hundred dollars on this elegant bed.

Tip #9 – Surround Yourself with Things That Are Important To You

The most beautiful homes are not those that have the most expensive things, but those that tell a good story. To feel connected with your environment, you have to surround yourself with things that are meaningful to you. It could be gifts, travel memorabilia, or things that represent your dreams.

For example, if you dream of owning a beach resort one day, you can surround your home with shells and beach fabrics. If you like to travel to Santorini, well, you can paint your home blue and white and decorate it with Greek decor like pillars, blue throw pillows, or dainty hammocks.

If you are Spanish and living in New York, maybe you can surround your apartment with things that remind you of home such as mahogany furniture, colorful tiles, and big chandeliers.

When you surround yourself with things that are meaningful to you, you will feel happy just by looking at them.

Tip #10 – Less is More

It's good to be surrounded by beautiful things. But, too much of anything is not good. Having too many things around your house can make you feel stressed and suffocated. So, keep everything simple. Remember that in most cases, less is more.

Tip #11– Light Up

Denmark is one of the darkest countries in the world, literally. This is the reason why the Danes have mastered the art of interior lighting. If you're not a fan of candles, you can use artificial lighting to make your home cozier, warmer, and brighter. You can use a combination of floor lamps and table lamps. You can also use chandeliers to give your home a classier look.

Tip #12 – Recycle

Danes hate waste. While it is important to throw away the things that you do not use anymore, it's a good idea to recycle some of your old things. For example, you can turn old bed sheets into new drapes. You can also use old wine glasses and bottles as flower vases.

Remember that living in a cozy home does not only make you feel happy, it also makes you relaxed. So, invest time and money into your home. Turn it into something that you truly want to go home to after a long and stressful day at work.

Creating a cozy home will not only help relieve stress, it can also increase the level of your happiness and self-satisfaction.

Cuddle With Your Loved One

There are only a few things that feel better than cuddling with your loved one. When you wake up in the morning, take time to cuddle with your partner. There's nothing more "hygge" than holding your partner in your arms on a cold winter day.

Hygge is all about getting cozy. It is about enjoying the little things in life and embracing everything that life has to offer.

6 - Get Physical: The Wonders of Exercise

You may think that hygge is just all about lounging around and getting cozy on a soft sofa. But, it is more than that. Hygge is about doing things that make you happy. It is about practicing mindfulness and living in the moment.

Certain physical exercises employ the principles of hygge. These exercises do not only improve your health, but they also allow you to live in the moment and help improve your mind and body connection.

Regular exercise can help you control your weight and could reduce the risk of cardiovascular diseases. It can improve your mental health and helps you shake off stress. It also increases your energy so you can do the things that you love often.

Practice Tai Chi

Tai Chi is a famous Chinese martial art. It is non-competitive and it includes various gentle movements that can do wonders to your body. This exercise is a powerful mindfulness practice that can help reduce stress and increase your physical and mental stamina.

Tai Chi was founded by a Taoist monk named Zhang San-feng. It incorporates the teachings and principles of Confucianism and Taoism.

This amazing exercise puts you in a good mood. It decreases the symptoms of anxiety, stress, and depression. It improves your agility, balance, and flexibility. It reduces inflammation and the symptoms of various diseases such as diabetes, chronic heart failure, fibromyalgia, depression, and Parkinson's disease.

Tai Chi is an inexpensive exercise. In fact, you can find free classes in some public parks. This exercise does not only reduce stress, it also expands your mind and allows you to learn more about the rich culture of the East.

Discover the Wonders of Yoga

Yoga is becoming more and more popular in the west these days. It helps reduce anxiety, stress, and depression. It may not have a Danish origin, but it certainly fits the concept of hygge.

Yoga keeps you grounded and helps you get in touch with yourself. It allows you to live in the moment and listen to your body. This powerful exercise calms down your nerves and increases your focus.

So, when you have a hard time concentrating on the task at hand because of too much stress, you have to practice yoga.

7 - Yoga poses that have almost the same effect as anti-depressant pills

Number One – Balasana or Child Pose

This is a transition yoga pose that relaxes your entire body. It is also an effective remedy for back pain and stiff neck. This pose has a strong restorative and healing power. To do this, kneel on your mat and rest your buttocks on your feet.

Take a deep breath and slowly lean forward and bring your head in front of your knees. Extend your arms in front of you and rest your palms on the mat. Hold this pose for at least one minute to reap its relaxing effect.

Number 2 – Adho Mukha Savasana or Downward Dog

This pose improves the blood circulation in your body. It relieves neck pain and it prevents the development of bone diseases. It releases stress and tension in your body and it is easy to do, too. Simply start on all fours. Then slowly, lift your buttocks and navel up so your body forms a reverse "v" shape.

Number 3 – Setu Bandha Sarvangasana or Bridge Pose

This pose does more than relieving stress. It also helps you lose weight. This pose improves the quality of your sleep and it boosts your metabolism. To do this, lie on your back with your hands on your side.

Take a deep breath and slowly lift your chest, buttocks, and knees from your yoga mat. Place your hands on your ankles and lock your chin. Hold this pose for thirty to sixty seconds. Release and repeat ten times.

Number 4 – Cat Pose

Premenstrual syndrome or PMS is a primary cause of stress for many women. It is painful, and it can negatively affect your mood and productivity. The cat pose stretches your spine and it helps remove the tension.

To do this, start on all fours. Take a deep breath and slowly lift your lower back, tucking your stomach in. Hold this for a few seconds and then release. Do this a couple of times a day to ease the tension in your body.

Number 5 – Savasana or the Corpse Pose

This is the simplest yoga pose and it is the most relaxing, too. This pose relaxes every part of your body. It lowers your blood pressure and it calms your nerves. This pose also improves the quality of your sleep and it relaxes your mind.

After a long day at work, lie down on your back with your feet slightly apart. Place your arms on your side, palms up. Close your eyes and take deep breaths. Stay in this position for at least ten minutes, but try not to fall asleep. You can do this pose after an intense yoga session.

Pilates

Pilates is a lot similar to yoga. In fact, it is a combination of ballet, calisthenics, and ballet. If you're experiencing back pain from sitting in front of the computer all day, you should try this exercise.

This incredible exercise was created and named after Joseph Pilates in the early 20th century. It employs the posterior lateral breathing method which allows you to breathe deep into the back of your rib cage. This breathing technique is extremely relaxing and it helps release the tension from your body. It also improves your concentration and cognitive abilities.

Pilates is a great exercise for those who are trying to lose weight, too. It increases your stamina and flexibility. It also improves sports performance because it enhances the efficiency of your body movement. It can do wonders to your joints.

Pilates is a full body workout that will not only reduce stress, it also helps you achieve your fitness goals.

Running

When you are stressed out and depressed, the last thing you want to do is get out of bed and go for a run. But, running is an amazing natural anti-depressant.

If you still need a little convincing to try out running, well, it is a powerful weight loss tool. It strengthens and tones the legs and also builds your core muscle. Plus, it also boosts self-confidence.

Running is a good exercise that you can do with people that you love. You can run with your friends or with your partner. You can even create a running club in your office so you could run with your friends after work hours.

Kickboxing

You may think that kicking ass is not congruent with the cozy concept of hygge. But, kickboxing is relaxing and it also allows you to live in the moment. It increases your mindfulness and the mind-body connection.

Swimming

Swimming is not only a basic survival skill, it is also an exciting and fun exercise. It increases your arm strength and endurance and allows you to achieve your dream body.

Swimming is a stress-relieving exercise. It reduces depression and helps improve your mood. This amazing sport can clear your head. The alternating relaxation and stretch of your skeletal muscles while breathing can trigger biochemical changes in your brain the same way that yoga does. It is also a repetitive exercise that can put you in a meditative state and relax your entire body.

So, after a long day at work, go to a nearby pool, if you don't have one and swim for thirty to sixty minutes to reap the maximum benefits of this amazing exercise.

Biking

It's no a secret that many Danes living in Copenhagen bike to work or school. Biking can save you a lot of gas money and has various health benefits, too. Like many other physical exercises, biking helps you burn calories and lose weight.

It also improves the quality of your sleep and according to a group of scientists from the University of Illinois, it makes you smarter because it improves the blood flow to the brain. It also improves your sex life and your work efficiency.

Like running, biking is a fun activity that you can do with your friends and loved ones.

Rowing

Rowing is a great aerobic exercise that helps you lose weight. It is also a great upper body workout that tones your chest and arms. It increases your endurance. It is convenient and affordable. You do not have to break the bank to do this exercise. It is surprisingly fun and it helps reduce stress.

Dancing

Dancing is fun. It improves your muscle strength and is a good skill to have. It improves your physical fitness and psychological well-being. It also improves your social skills and helps you become more connected with yourself and others.

If you're stressed out, enroll in dance classes. You can try Zumba or its classic form - ballroom dancing. You can also try belly dancing, hip hop, jazz, salsa, tap dancing, square dancing, and pole dancing.

Regular exercise can do wonders to your mind and body. If you truly want to shake off stress and positively change your life, get moving. Your future self will thank you for it.

Hygge and Time Management

Denmark has one of the most stable economies in the world. So, you'd think that they are obsessed with work like the Japanese people or the Americans? As it turns out, they do not spend a lot of time at work. This does not mean that they have bad work ethics. They just mastered the art of time management.

You see, hygge is about being mindful and making the most out of your time. It is about creating a balance in your life. So, if you want to avoid stress, you should follow these hygge time management tips:

Tip #1: Leave Work On Time

Danes are hard working. What's interesting is that they leave work on time. Working for 12 hours a day can wreak havoc on your health. It can cause mental fog and reduce your work efficiency and productivity. In order to live an awesome stress-free life, you have to do what the Danes do and leave work on time.

Doing allows you to maintain a healthy work-life balance. It helps you focus on important tasks and it improves your discipline. If you have to leave work on time all the time, you'll most likely drop your procrastinating habits and avoid distractions. You'll also find new ways to get things done.

This time management strategy makes you a better person

because you'll have time to take care of yourself, cultivate your mind, and spend time with the people you love.

Tip #2: Write An Effective "To Do" List

We all know the importance of a "To Do" list but let's face it. Not all "to do" lists are created equal. To make the most out of your day, you have to limit the items in your "to do" list and stick to at most, three important tasks per day. This allows you to focus on things that really matters. This should include important tasks such as project proposals, reports, important client meetings, and employee engagement.

You can create a separate list of errands and trivial tasks such as unimportant client callback, status updates, and emails. You can do these tasks after you've completed the three most important tasks.

You see, email can take up a lot of your day and it is distracting. So, unless you're a virtual assistant, email marketer, or email specialist, you have to manage your time well and check your email twice a day. This will help you manage your time well and focus on more important and pressing things.

Tip #3: Wake Up Early

Waking up is hard to do, especially during the cold and gloomy winter time. Many Danes have a hard time waking up early. But, highly successful and creative people such as the famous philosopher Søren Kierkegaard try to wake up before 6 am. Waking up early can help you maximize your time and can minimize stress, too.

Tip #4: Stop Being A Perfectionist

Danes are good at a lot of things, but they do not sweat the small stuff. They are not concerned with how other people see them. Because of this, they are not as obsessed with perfection as Americans, the Brits, or even the high-achieving Asians. The Danes understand that it's useless to aim for perfection, so they do their best instead. To avoid stress, stop aiming for perfection. Believe that your best is good enough.

Tip #5: Just Do It

Procrastination will make you feel stressed and can cause complications in your career and life. If you want to live a stress-free life, you have to decide to get the task done and just do it.

Tip #6: Manage the Distractions

Leaving on time is difficult for a lot of people because of distractions. So, to get things done and beat stress, you have to beat procrastination and learn to manage distractions. You can do this by turning off your phone when you are doing an important and urgent task. You can also block distracting websites such as Twitter, Facebook, and Instagram during work hours.

Tip #7: Time Box Your Tasks

You'll most likely do multiple tasks in a day, so it is a good idea to time box your tasks. This technique increases your productivity and helps you meet deadlines. For example, you can box Task A from 10 am to 10:30 am. This will create a strong sense of urgency and will keep you from procrastinating.

Tip #8: Organize Your Workspace

To enjoy the maximum benefits of hygge, you have to make

your work space cozy. Clutter is distracting. In order to increase your productivity and achieve work life balance, take the time to purge your office and get rid of the things that you no longer want or need.

You can also light lemon or jasmine scented candle while working. These scents can sharpen your mind and can increase your productivity right away.

Tip #9: Spend Time For Self-Improvement

One of the most important keys to productivity is self-improvement. When you hone your skills, you get to complete your tasks faster. For example, if you want to finish your report faster, then you should take the time to learn Microsoft Excel shortcuts. This could save you a lot of time and energy.

Time management is not only a valuable life skill that everyone must learn. It is also a powerful "hygge" skill that can help you achieve a balanced and happy life. So, prioritize your tasks, focus on tasks that yield more results, and Leave work on time. It cannot get more Danish than that.

8 - The Power of Connection: Spending Time with Those who Matter

The Danes live in the Nordic region and they are naturally independent. They do not expect their parents or spouses to provide for them. But, they also recognize the power of connection. They understand the importance of relationships.

Spend Time With Your Loved Ones

Do not work too hard to the point that you forget who you are doing it for in the first place. No matter how busy your day or week is, do not forget to spend time with the people who matter to you.

Here's a list of tips that can help you do that:

Number 1 – Eat With Them

Spend at least one meal a day with your loved ones. It can be your kids, your spouse, or friends.

Number 2 – Include Your Loved Ones In Your Weekends

Do you surf during weekends? Well, make it a family activity and include your loved ones. You can also surf with your friends. Fun activities are twice the fun if you do it with people who are close to your heart.

Number 3- Take Vacations with People Who Matter To You

Beautiful vacation destinations like Paris, Rome, Cancun, Miami, and Sydney are more beautiful when you visit them with your loved ones. So, plan your next vacation with family or friends.

Number 4- Send Your Loved Ones Random Text Messages

Sometimes, we can't physically spend time with our loved ones. When that happens, send them loving and funny text messages to show them that you are thinking of them. You can randomly ask your children how they are doing at school or send a sexy message to your spouse. It would surely make their day.

Number 5 – Throw Surprise Birthday Parties for Your Friends

The Danes may be all "chill" and "relaxed", but they love to party, too. To make your close friends special, throw surprise birthday parties for them. This will surely make their day. If this is too much, you can simply buy them flowers or a gift.

You can also connect with your friends and loved ones by telling them what you like most about them. This will not only make them smile, it will also make their day. Giving genuine compliments to your loved ones can help strengthen your relationships with them.

Enjoy Quality Time with Your Pets

Your pets are more than just your friends or companions. They are your family, too. Having a pet improves the overall quality of your life. They decrease your stress and blood pressure. They improve your mood and help ease your pain and/or sadness.

8 - THE POWER OF CONNECTION: SPENDING TIME WITH THOSE WHO MATTER

Your pets can help you get over your pain and they can help heal your broken heart. They will love you unconditionally. So, take time to play with them. This can bring immeasurable joy into your life.

Celebrate your individualism, but remember to spend time with your loved ones. You'd find great joy in being connected with people who love, support, and accept you.

9 - Learning The Art of Unplugging

The world has too much noise, even virtual noise. The internet is filled with lies, pressures, and drama. To practice hygge, you must master the art of unplugging and digital detox.

Digital detox helps reduce stress and clears the mind. It also frees up a lot of your time and allows you to reboot. Digital detox helps improve your optimism and reduces stress in your body. But, unplugging from the physical or digital world is not as easy as you think. It is extremely challenging. To temporarily disconnect from the world and achieve inner peace, follow these tips:

Tip #1 – Practice Meditation

Meditation is a powerful relaxation tool that you can use to relieve stress. It relaxes your mind and improves your cognitive function. It also helps you achieve something that we all want – peace of mind. If you're stressed out and you've had enough of the external and internal noise, sit in a quiet place and just pay attention to your breath. This mindfulness practice is powerful.

Tip#2 – Turn Off Your Phone Every Once In a While

If you want to live in the moment, you have to turn off your phone during meal times and instead have a conversation with your loved ones. You also need to turn off your phone when you're on a date with your spouse or partner. This is to ensure that you are giving him/her your full, undivided attention.

Tip#3 – Do Not Place a TV or Computer in Your Room

Your bedroom is a place of rest. So, do not place a TV or laptop inside your bedroom. Also, try not to check social media in the morning.

Tip#4 – Allot Time for Social Media Use

To control your social media usage, schedule your social media use and limit it to at least thirty minutes a day. This will maximize your productivity and help reduce the noise in your life.

Tip #5 – Go For a Walk

When you feel the urge to check on your social media accounts, go for a walk instead. You can walk around your office or neighborhood. This is a good physical exercise and can also help you curb the urge to just lurk on social media.

Unplugging does not only reduce stress, it also clears your mind and helps you manage negative emotions such as envy, anger, and resentment.

10 - Hygge and The Healing Magic of Music

Music touches your soul. It can invoke different kinds of emotions. So, if you're stressed out and a little depressed, listen to good music. Music heals different types of emotional stress. It eases anxiety and is a potent treatment for mild depression.

Music improves health by reducing your cortisol levels. It helps you sleep better and makes you happier. According to a study conducted at Georgia Tech University, music could help control one's appetite.

Listening to music also strengthens your memory and makes you smarter. A study in Japan showed that people who listen to music have better test results than those who don't. Another study also shows that children who take music lessons have higher IQs. Music is so powerful that it can reduce the symptoms of Alzheimer's.

Music can ease different kinds of pain. It motivates you to work out and maintain a healthy lifestyle and also improves your sleep quality. It can also help you cope up with high-pressure situations.

So, if you're feeling stressed or sick, put on an earphone and listen to relaxing music. Listen to music that changes your current emotional state.

If you are angry, listen to music that reduces your heart rate such as "Feels" by Giraffage, "Feel Flows" by Slow Magic, "Silver" by Caribou, "Your Bones" by Beach House, "Kimekai" by Le Loyon, "Day Dream" by Nitin Sawhmeny, "Woman" by Rhye, and "Show Me Love" by Hundred Waters. These songs have sound frequencies that will naturally reduce your stress and anxiety.

If you're sad or depressed, you can listen to inspiring songs like "Fight Song" by Rachel Platten, "I Choose" by India Arie, "Swim" by Jack Mannequin, "Now Is The Start" by A Fine Frenzy, "Dream Big" by Ryan Shupe & the Rubberband, "I'm Good" by the Mowgils, "Survivor" by Destiny's Child, and "I Will Survive" by Gloria Gaynor. These songs have powerful lyrics that can lift up your spirit.

You can also listen to songs with happy and upbeat melodies such as "Sugar Sugar" by The Archies, "Good Day Sunshine" by the Beatles", "Blessed" by Brett Dennen, "Rainbow Connection" by Jason Mraz, "Everybody" by Ingrid Michaelson, and "First Day of My Eyes" by Bright Eyes.

Music is a powerful tool that you can use to improve your life. If you are feeling a bit overwhelmed with the pressures of life, simply put on your headset and listen to powerful music.

11 - Enjoy Life's Simple Pleasures

When you first learn about the hygge lifestyle, you may say "But, I am not rich. I cannot afford this lifestyle". This is an understandable concern. But, hygge is not about living a luxurious life. It is about enjoying life's little pleasures. It is about appreciating what you have.

Adopt the Attitude of Gratitude

Gratitude is powerful because it cultivates contentment. It allows you to appreciate what you have and it helps you avoid negative feelings such as envy or resentment.

Gratitude raises your energetic vibrations and makes you happier. It also makes you more resilient. This makes it easier for you to deal with life's difficulties and stress.

Take time to write thank you notes to people who have been nice to you and who have made your life easier – your co-workers, spouse, children, parents, siblings, friends, and even your cleaning lady.

Having a grateful heart makes you happier and less suscept-ible to stress.

Take Time to Smell the Roses

This may sound cliche, but to avoid stress, you have to slow down and appreciate the beauty all around you. Take time to walk around the park each morning and appreciate the beauty and the scent of the flowers. While you drive to work, look around you and notice the beauty of your surroundings.

This exercise does not only relieve stress but also makes you calmer and happier.

Eat Good Food

The Danes are not as diet obsessed as Americans. They eat good food, but in moderation. If you are working too hard lately, treat yourself to some good food. Eat cheese, a little chocolate, and drink some good wine. You've been working too hard and doing the best that you can, so lay back and enjoy good food with friends.

You do not have to eat something expensive. You can simply enjoy a cup of ice cream or a slice of blueberry cheesecake.

Plan Spontaneous Trips

You do not have to go to Paris or other expensive tourist destinations. You can simply travel to a nearby city or go to the beach. You can also plan "budget travels" and go to beautiful but cheap destinations.

Take time to enjoy the small pleasures in life, such as the smell of the rain, a sinful can of Pringles, some loose change in your pocket, or big servings of French fries.

Play a Game

Computer games are getting bad press lately. But, the truth is, they can help you blow off some steam. They can help you relax after a long day at work and even increase your creativity. So, after a long day at work, sit back, put your feet up, and play a good game.

Play in the Rain

Playing in the rain may be a childish thing but it can bring you great joy and can help reduce stress, too. You can do this with your friends or kids.

Simple yet pleasurable activities

- If you're a How I Met Your Mother Fan, buy a yellow umbrella.

- Walk around the park and bring your camera. Take pictures of flowers or squirrels. This will help you practice mindfulness and makes you appreciate the beauty of your surroundings.

- Use a sweet-smelling shampoo.

- Walk barefoot on a beach.

- Practice mindfulness and chew your food well. Eat like you're a food critic.

- Place fresh flowers in the middle of your dining table.

- Watch the videos of a comedian named Jo Koy on YouTube. He may not be George Carlin, but he has brilliant jokes.

- Bake delicious brownies.

- Enjoy the scent of your food before you eat them.

- Plan your fantasy vacation. You don't have to actually

do it. Psychologists say that planning your dream vacation has almost the same effect as actually taking the vacation.

- Sing in the shower. This will help you release all the tension.

- Laugh uncontrollably.

- Kiss your partner in public.

- Make out with your partner in weird places like a wedding reception or a library.

- Place rubber duckies in your bathtub and play with them.

- Wear a color coordinated outfit to surprise everyone.

- Make a donation to a charitable organization. This can make you feel good and allows you to be a part of a cause.

- Build a small bed for your cat.

- Go to a cat café. If you're a dog person, go to a dog café.

- Buy flowers for your mother.

- Blow bubbles with your adult friends.

- Tickle your partner.

- Listen to good music.

- Eat a chocolate candy after a grueling meeting with clients.

- Stay indoors wearing a large shirt and loose sweat-pants.

- Organize a treasure hunt with your friends.

- Drink a cup of hot pumpkin soup with cinnamon on a cold winter night.

- Sleep during rainy days.

- Master the art of telling a good story.

- Sit on a park bench and do people-watching.

- Buy a balloon and release it.

- Build a sandcastle.

- Sit by the fireplace and keep yourself warm during

cold nights.

- Chew a peppermint gum.

- Go on a date with your special someone.

- Watch the snow fall.

- Enjoy a good laugh with your friends.

- Make a stranger smile.

- Watch the sunset and the sunrise. Get out of your house or your car and simply enjoy the sight of the sun.

- Get a glamor shot. You deserve to feel like a super-model even for a day.

- Watch a magic show and believe in magic like a child.

- Call an estranged friend.

- Plant herbs in colorful flower pots.

- Eat a cup of Greek yogurt with fresh berries.

- Go Salsa dancing on a weeknight.

- Dance while you're cleaning your bedroom or living

room.

- Go to museums and public libraries.

- Bake a pie.

- Buy stationery and write letters.

- Swim in a lake.

- Watch the clouds move.

- Learn a new skill like crocheting or woodworking.

- Hold hands with your lover.

- Go to the farmer's market and buy fresh fruits and vegetables.

- Get a foot massage.

- Kiss your puppy.

- Get out of your car and enjoy the sight of city lights.

- Be silly.

- Go to a Halloween party as your favorite superhero.

- Open an expensive bottle of champagne and drink it

while watching your favorite movie on Netflix.

• Raise your wine glass and say "cheers to a good life".

You do not have to do something expensive or grand. Enjoying the simple pleasures in life helps you deal with stress more effectively. It makes you happier and more content.

12 - The Magic of Aromatherapy

If you're stressed, then you may want to harness the benefits of aromatherapy. Aromatherapy did not originate in Denmark, but it fits into the huge lifestyle. It is a practice that's used by ancient Romans, Greeks, Egyptians, Indians, and Chinese. It involves the use of essential oils, aroma lamps, vaporizer, and carrier oils.

Aromatherapy reduces stress and helps fight depression. It helps you manage pain and improves your blood pressure.

Here's a list of essential oils that you can use to cozy up and reduce stress:

Lavender

This essential oil has a calming effect. It helps you relax after a long day and achieve inner peace amidst all the external noise and pressures. It reduces anxiety and negative thoughts. It also helps you have a good night sleep.

Rose

This oil has a sweet and seductive scent that can relieve depression and anxiety. This amazing essential oil has an anti-inflammatory effect and it keeps you young, too. So, if you want to look young and live a stress-free life, use rose-scented candles. You can also spray a little rose oil on your pillow before you go to sleep.

Ylang ylang

This is an expensive and exotic essential oil that's used in popular perfumes. It is so powerful that it can reduce the symptoms of depression and anxiety. It calms agitation and nervous palpitations. It also encourages courage, cheerfulness, and optimism. This oil blends well with lavender and bergamot oils.

Chamomile

This relaxing oil has a soothing scent. It reduces overthinking, worries, and anxiety. It has the power to shut down all the noise in your head and achieve inner peace.

Bergamot

This oil is extremely calming and can help you control your emotions. If you're stressed, angry, and irritable all the time, you should try this essential oil.

Lemon

This oil is extremely refreshing. It calms your nerves and it can strengthen your immune system. It can even help you lose weight.

When you're stressed or freaking out, you can sniff these oils. You can also add them to your bath or you can place them in an oil burner with a diffuser or candle. You can even use them as perfumes.

13 - Celebrate Your Life

Your life is a blessing. If you had a bad experience after another, sit back and celebrate your life. Celebrating your life helps you deal with difficulties and stress, and increases abundance and the flow of blessings. It brings more happiness into your life and brings in great opportunities. It increases your vibrational frequency so it allows you to attract more opportunities.

Celebrating your life also makes you more grounded. It helps you realize that you are blessed and so it increases your resiliency. It also makes you feel more in control of your life.

Here's how you can celebrate life on a daily basis:

Be grateful

Gratitude allows you to celebrate and enjoy all that you have. It makes you realize that you have more than enough. So, every day, after you wake up, think of the things that you are grateful for. It could be anything. It could be the roof over your head or your soft and fluffy bed. It could be your lover, your job, or your money in the bank.

Gratitude increases contentment and makes you happier. It

also reduces materialism because you'll realize that you have almost everything you need and you don't need that Ferrari or that Louis Vuitton bag.

Help Others

This may sound strange, but you can celebrate your life by helping others. If you were blessed with financial abundance or intelligence, then, by all means, share those blessings with others. Try to help other people whenever you can. You do not have to give them money or material things. You can give them your time or you can share your expertise.

Throw Parties On Your Birthday

You should celebrate your life daily. But, the best day to celebrate your life is on your birthday. So, host a party on your birthday. You can take your loved ones out to a fancy dinner or you can have a spa party. You can even have a basketball party. Whatever works for you. Celebrating your birthday is a good way to celebrate your awesomeness.

Treat Yourself

It's not bad to celebrate your wins. To truly enjoy life, you have to treat yourself and celebrate your wins. You've completed a task? Great! Eat a scoop of your favorite ice cream. You've passed your exam? Awesome! Go buy yourself a new pair of shoes. Take time to celebrate all your wins – big or small.

You are a good person and you are awesome. You deserve those little treats, too. And if you can afford it, give yourself big treats from time to time. Buy yourself expensive things.

Love Yourself Like Crazy

Loving yourself is not narcissism. It is a necessity. To live a happy life, you have to appreciate yourself. You have to believe that you deserve all the good things in this world.

Take time to look in the mirror and appreciate your appearance. You are more attractive than what you'd like to believe. Every morning, look in the mirror and appreciate your hair, your eyes, and your body. Fall in love with yourself.

Also, learn to forgive yourself. So what if you made bad decisions in the past? Everyone makes mistakes. Get over your bad decisions. You are not your mistakes. You are not your bad decisions. So, stop blaming yourself. Stop hating yourself. Start embracing yourself for who you are – flaws and all.

Allow Others to Pamper You

To celebrate your life, let other people celebrate you. Allow your loved ones to spoil and pamper you. Let them give you the world. Graciously accept gifts and compliments because you deserve them.

Do The Things That You Want to Do

A lot of us do what we are expected to do. Only a few people really do what they want to do. To celebrate your life and reduce stress, focus on projects that you are passionate about. You do not have to leave your day job. You can spend your free time doing things that make your heart sing. You can paint, write songs, surf, or sew clothes. You deserve to do the things that make you happy.

Dress To Kill

If you plan to celebrate yourself each day, you have to dress the part. The Danes love comfortable but fashionable clothes. So, put on your best clothes and look your best each day. Wearing good clothes help decrease stress because it makes you feel good. You don't have to buy expensive ones.

You can find a lot of cheap but stylish clothes at the mall.

Take Risks

One of the best ways to celebrate your life is to do something extraordinary. Celebrate what your body can do by doing complicated yoga poses. You can also celebrate your life by doing adventurous stuff like climbing up the mountain or hiking in the cold mountains of Iceland. You can also do something very Danish like watch the Northern Lights on a cold winter night.

Take risks at work, too, and make bold business decisions. Taking risks do not guarantee huge returns. But, if you do it right, it can change your life.

Taking risks increases your self-confidence and it empowers you to go beyond your limits. It also helps you learn new skills and see new opportunities. In the end, it helps you get what you want. It helps you stand out too.

Celebrate Other People

One of the best ways to celebrate your life is to celebrate others. Take time to appreciate the people around you and celebrate them. You don't have to do something grand, you can simply give them a simple gift or a genuine compliment. This will definitely make their day.

Also, avoid envy. Envy stresses you out and it can drain you. Learn to silence your inner green monster and master the art of being happy for others. Do not roll your eyes when you see someone posting about their achievements on Facebook. Congratulate them instead and let them know that you are happy for them.

You can also celebrate other people by letting them shine. If you're a leader, make it a habit of putting the spotlight on someone else.

Also, be sensitive to other people's needs and feelings. Listen to them and let them know that their concerns and opinions are important, too.

You only have one life, so celebrate it!

14 - Conclusion

Thank you again for downloading this book!

The Danes may look quiet and reserved. But, they are extremely happy and satisfied with their lives using hygge. I hope that this book was able to help you cope with stress and build a happier and more fulfilling life.

Let's recap a little bit, to reduce stress in your life, you have to:

- Make your home clutter-free.

- Cozy up in your bed during a rainy day.

- Establish drama-free relationships.

- Stay away from toxic people.

- Surround yourself with happy and supportive people.

- Take a deep breath and live in the present moment.

- Celebrate your life.

- Enjoy the simple things in life.

- Do a digital detox.

14 - CONCLUSION

- Slow down and appreciate the simple pleasures.

I hope that you use this book to completely remove stress from your life. I also hope that you use what you've learned in this book to improve yourself and build stronger relationships.

Thank you and good luck!

Thank You

As we reach the end of this book, I want to say thanks for reading this book.

I want to get this information out to as many people as possible. If you found this book helpful, I would greatly appreciate you leaving me a review. This helps others find the book as well.

Disclaimer

This document is geared towards providing exact and reliable information in regards to the topic and issue covered. The publication is sold on the idea that the publisher is not required to render an accounting, officially permitted, or otherwise, qualified services. If advice is necessary, legal, financial, medical or professional, a practiced individual in the profession should be ordered.

This information is not presented by a financial or medical practitioner and is for entertainment, educational and informational purposes only. The content is not intended as a substitute for professional medical advice, diagnosis, or treatment. Always seek the advice of your physician or other qualified health care provider with any questions you may have regarding a medical condition. Never disregard professional medical advice or delay in seeking it because of something you have read.

The information provided herein is stated to be truthful and consistent, in that any liability, in terms of inattention or otherwise, by any usage or abuse of any policies, processes, or directions contained within is the solitary and utter responsibility of the recipient reader. Under no circumstances will any legal responsibility or blame be held against the

DISCLAIMER

publisher for any reparation, damages, or monetary loss due to the information herein, either directly or indirectly.

Last Updated: 11.Jun.2017

CPSIA information can be obtained
at www.ICGtesting.com
Printed in the USA
LVHW080553310123
738235LV00001B/27